UNDERSTANDING FAITH

Understanding Christianity

UNDERSTANDING FAITH

SERIES EDITOR: PROFESSOR FRANK WHALING

Available

Understanding Judaism, Jeremy Rosen
Understanding Sikhism, Owen Cole

Forthcoming

Understanding Buddhism, Perry Schmidt-Leukel
Understanding Hinduism, Frank Whaling

UNDERSTANDING FAITH

SERIES EDITOR: PROFESSOR FRANK WHALING

Understanding Christianity

Gilleasbuig Macmillan

DUNEDIN ACADEMIC PRESS

EDINBURGH

Published by
Dunedin Academic Press Ltd
Hudson House
8 Albany Street
Edinburgh EH1 3QB
Scotland

ISBN 1 903765 22 6
ISSN 1744-5833

BRITISH LIBRARY CATALOGUING IN PUBLICATION DATA
A catalogue record for this book is available from the British Library.

Set in 10/12pt Plantin with Stone Sans display
by Makar Publishing Production, Edinburgh.
Cover design by Mark Blackadder.

Printed and bound in Great Britain by
Cromwell Press

CONTENTS

Prelude

For thirty-five years I have been employed as a minister. You might call me a pastor or preacher or priest. Each of these four words – minister, pastor, preacher, and priest – suggests something about the nature of Christianity, the subject of this book. The book is not about the profession of being a parson, a member of the clergy. It is emphatically not written from any assumption that the clergy are a superior form of Christian belief and practice. It remains the fact, however, that being a minister is what I am, and, although the prominence of the clergy in the history of our religion cannot be ignored and will be faced in this book as a fact and a problem, I write from where I am. The word minister suggests two things. The first is that the clergy are there to serve, to help, to give service. Like comparable officials in other communities and traditions of faith or religion, they are in office to provide facilities and benefits for people which they, the people, regard as things they need, or wish, or ought, to have. The second thing the word suggests is that the principal ministry in Christianity is the ministry of Jesus Christ. It will come as no surprise that Jesus Christ is central to Christianity, and that centrality is affirmed both by using a word which means servant to make connection with him, and by the wide acceptance that all Christian people, and not just the professional ministry or priesthood, see themselves as trying to follow the example of Jesus, and even sharing in his ministry.

The word pastor, which means shepherd, immediately points to the communal character of the Christian, as of other, religions. Caring for one another may be said to be a defining feature of any community inasmuch as it is a community, and not a collection of detached individuals, and the social expression of Christian faith has always been regarded as deeply important. Sometimes the community, the church, has been seen as a clearly defined unit, while at other times the unit of communal awareness and mutual care has been the entire population of a place, the parish. For much of Christian history any distinction between the community of the church and the community of the whole population was blurred or practically non-existent. Some people find it easier than others to define the church or say who are its members; at this stage it is sufficient to accept the central significance of church to Christianity.

One of the principal elements in a minister's work is preaching. The word preacher can be taken to cover efforts made to understand the faith, to help professed believers to have a fuller understanding of their faith, to proclaim and spread the faith among those who are not professed believers, and to suggest practical implications of Christian belief, in personal behaviour, social and national priorities, and the efforts of the peoples of the world to inhabit the world together. In all these aspects, the Bible is deeply important, as well as the doctrines which churches hold to be particularly important (it being generally held that after the Bible, the Apostles' and Nicene Creeds occupy especially honoured places). Closely related to preaching is artistic expression, the use of music and painting and sculpture, as well as verbal expression in poetry and other writing.

The word priest suggests the liturgical function of the minister, thus connecting Christian practitioners to those whose function it has been to act ceremonially in ordered ritual according to the traditions and rules of different religions. Here the priest is sometimes seen as dominating the proceedings and the people who are present, but also as servant, a facilitator rather than a master. Worship, or church services, are more than the expression of beliefs. They are more fundamental than beliefs, and may properly take precedence over them (though a culture which elevates individual opinion to a high level, in theory at least, finds such a judgement difficult at times, or even offensive). Worship is the home territory of religious believing, and private worship, however significant it can undoubtedly be, cannot for long replace the communal act of people worshipping together.

Thus, the four words or titles covering the profession of the writer of these pages suggest to us central ingredients of Christianity. I make the disclaimer again, however, that Christianity is not chiefly for or about the clergy. Like all religions, its followers are able to see its scope of significance as being very wide indeed, including, just possibly, everything.

Christianity began in the Middle East, on the continent of Asia, a little under two thousand years ago. For much of the time since then, roughly fifteen hundred years, it has been the established religion of the continent of Europe. Now, at the beginning of the twenty-first century, a gigantic shift is occurring in a southerly direction; and it has been predicted that by 2025 the world's Christian population will be 2.6 billion, making it the world's largest faith by far, and that the proportion of 'non-Latino whites' will possibly be one in five. When you consider that in Europe and North America a growing proportion of churchgoers comes from a non-European, non-white background (it is said that about half the number of people attending church in

London is black), the shift from traditional European culture is all the more marked. It seems a good time to ask some questions about the Christian faith.

We in Britain have grown accustomed to the decline of the Christian churches, both in the sense that surveys of church attendance and attachment show that the numbers are going down, and also in the assumptions made in print and conversation that this is a weak, even pathetic time for the churches. The view, widely held in the past, that modernity and secularisation had slowly but surely eroded belief and undermined the bases of the church's existence over a period of centuries is open to challenge, especially by the fact that the decline in numbers has been large and significant only within the past thirty years approximately. At the same time, therefore, as numbers of church people are increasing rapidly in the southern continents, attachment to the faith in its old heartlands appears to be getting thinner and thinner. It is also, therefore, an interesting time to ask questions about the nature of Christianity.

It is, I think, worth asking how far Christianity is one thing, or one set of ideas, or one system of life and thought. There is a great risk that life will lose its colour and its smell when it becomes an entry in an encyclopaedia. Think of a person who has lost the way to a big house in a beautiful garden with a fine broad gateway and a straight avenue from the gate to the house. If that person, having failed to find the big gate, notices a little gate round the corner, or a gap in the hedge, or even a ditch running out under the hedge, should that person spurn these lesser entries because the big main entrance is out of sight? Sometimes the peripheral aspects of an area of life offer entry points leading to a full involvement with that area. That is good to bear in mind when people wish to catch something of the heart of a religion. The encyclopaedia may not be the best place to start. The little gaps in the hedge may offer points of authentic entry – not immediately granting the whole reality, but including the colour and smell, the atmosphere, a genuine sip of the water which fills the whole fountain.

The point I am making is, I am sure, true of all religions; but since it is Christianity that we are considering, church members will have their own local and personal small items of more or less peripheral character which somehow contain the whole in the part, or at least allow the part to point to the whole, or be a reminder of the whole. Here is one such list:

> a stained-glass window in church
> Caravaggio's *Conversion of St Paul*
> a bedtime prayer said in childhood

the tune of an evening hymn
the legends of local saints
the sight of an old man, head bowed in prayer
Annunciation, by Fra Angelico

What does understanding Christianity mean? Does it mean the following of an argument, so that we will be able to appreciate how the statements in the creeds, and other statements of belief, were produced on the assumption that certain primary claims were true? Might it refer to our having some useful knowledge available to us, which would help us to explain some of the important events in the history of the church, such as the controversy about icons, the Reformation, and Papal Infallibility? Both these interpretations are reasonable, but there is a third: the sense of understanding which one person has about another person, which amounts to a sympathetic identification with the other, even when grounds for explanation of the other's words or conduct are lacking. Such sympathy can enable us to know what purpose a doctrine – or a hymn, or a holy picture – was intended to serve, even if we would not express it in that way, or even if we fail to see why that purpose was thought to be served in that way. Now, it can be uncommonly difficult to see the world through the eyes of someone you have known for years. How then are we to try to see the world through the eyes – the lenses, the perspectives – of Saint Paul or Saint Basil or Saint Augustine, of Luther or Wesley or John Paul II? In a short book of this nature, we cannot expect full scholarly treatment of the entire history of the Christian Church (or churches), though an effort will be made to tell something of the flesh-and-blood story of the faith, with specific summaries of the lives of some of the people who stand out, some of them as representative, and others as unrepresentative, of time and place, change and continuity.

Something, however, matters much more (to me, and I hope to others) than arriving at a sympathetic understanding of the past of Christianity. That something more is an understanding of the faith today, Christianity now. Such an understanding involves a devotion of much thought to the claims that are made; but it involves even more entering into the worship of the church and testing the liturgical activity of Christianity for useful authenticity. I recognise that for some people it will appear to be straightforward and sensible to take the view that you decide first that you can accept enough of the doctrine before you participate in the worship. That, I maintain, is giving doctrines and beliefs much too important a place in the Christian religion. Doctrinal statements are more or less useful summaries of ecclesiastical agreement about important elements in the faith; but what matters much more is that the elements to which the statements point work in worship to serve people and facilitate their expression of the real heart of Christian worship. (It strikes me that bothering about what you believe before trying the practice of worship is somewhat akin to reading everything you can about Scotch whisky with a view to reaching a decision about whether to drink it, but refusing even to sip the stuff until you have arrived at a firm position on the matter.)

I find it helpful to make a distinction between *believing that* and *believing in*. What matters in religious believing is not the holding of opinions on religious questions, but the practical exercise of trust as you face the future. It is the distinction between believing in the doctor, that is to say, trusting the doctor, and believing that the doctor exists, which is usually a quite pointless thing to think or say. While I recognise that the doctor is physical and visible, whereas God is usually held to be neither, I still think the comparison is helpful, in that it is the trusting sense of believing that matters, and not the sense of holding opinions on religious matters. I therefore wish my understanding of Christianity to take the form of its worship – the principal action of any religion – engaging me in ways that are deeply important.

I see religion as existing to serve life, and not to be a sealed and separate world existing for its own sake. Understanding Christianity, then, must find a living connection between the heart of religion and the most significant areas of our lives, whether individually or socially. Some years ago I read an article entitled 'Religion as a Leisure-Time Pursuit' which claimed, as I remember, that churchgoing had come to provide more or less the same benefits offered to people as golf, bridge, wine tasting, stamp collecting, or collecting rare first editions of books by obscure writers. Quite useful, and harmless, often with good consequences for mind or body, such pastimes would be regarded by their practitioners and others as optional extras in life, bringing attraction partly for that very reason, that they are not obligatory. The practice of religious duty would not have been regarded in this way by our ancestors. The very nature of leisure and leisure-time activities assumes a developed society with time, wealth and spare energy enough for such activities. A community lacking such things would not have treated religion as something they were too poor, too tired, or too busy to do. For most of the world, religious observance has not been an optional extra. For modern westerners not only is it optional, but there appears to be almost a sense of virtue in making religion a personal choice and not a communal duty (and some Christian preachers seem to promote such a perspective). Of course religious faith may involve, from time to time, personal decision, the arriving at some judgement of mind on some matter, and an act of will which may go against the mind of most or all other people. But for many, if not all, religious believing and belonging have their origin and their strengthening in the customs of upbringing and environment, in the culture of home and village and nation. I suspect that some in the modern western world feel rather embarrassed about the extent to which their church attachment is inherited and their religious practice continuous with the practice of parents and predecessors. Such embarrassment ought to be replaced by pride – so long as there is room left for challenging the inheritance and making one's own contribution to its development.

I say to people approaching first communion that the faith which matters to me is a continuing conversation between me and the faith of the church, rather like a seagull walking along a see-saw, backwards and forwards, one end of the see-saw being the church's faith, and the other mine. Neither is to be the sole basis of one's spiritual nourishment or judgement. The conversation between the two, like the seagull's walk, will tend to be unbalanced in one direction or the other. Perfect balance is not a sign of life, except possibly in the case of the bird.

To understand Christianity, therefore, will involve some knowledge of things past, but, more significantly, it will involve the awareness of its present practice, chiefly in sensing something of the ways in which Christian worship is related to the worshippers' perspective on life in general. It will be an understanding that takes into account the centrality of Jesus Christ and is aware of the rich diversity of insight, imagery, and narrative in the Bible.

A man once approached me in Jerusalem, offering his service as a guide. I asked him what his religion was. He replied, 'We are Arabs from here.' There could have been misunderstanding on the part of either or both of us; but his reply struck me as deeply significant. It said much about the nature of religious involvement for most people in most places in the history of the world: that people's religion was social (we); racial or tribal (Arabs); and geographical (here). Our world may be different from that of most of our forebears; but it is still an inadequate response to the Christian – or any – religion to amass some facts and then ask ourselves if we like them.

Approaching Understanding:
Going to Church

We might pause to consider the building. It may be a room with little to distinguish it from a hall used for teaching, card games or political rhetoric; or it may be one of the great buildings of the world, and unmistakably a church: Chartres Cathedral, or Lincoln, or St Mark's in Venice. It may be a white New England place of peace, purity, and piety, or a church in Switzerland with steep roof and high spire meeting the winter snow, with one of those great clock faces on the tower. It need not be ancient. You don't get ancient churches in sub-Saharan Africa, but you get full churches shaded from the African sun. All round the world these buildings stand, and most of them have been made to be different, holy places – and if they do not look holy to the eye of the stranger, the people who love them will see them as 'the very gate of heaven'. I have heard some people say in recent years that the building doesn't matter, what matters is the people. Doubtless they realise that many people do not share their view; but I wonder if they are also missing an element in religion that is very old, very basic: the setting apart of an area to be thenceforth regarded as sacred space, either enclosed as a building, or marked off in open country or forest. If Christianity is a religion, it inevitably has elements shared with other religions. Not every ingredient in religion will take on a distinctively Christian stamp, setting it apart from the ways in which other religions meet the same need or express the same feature of life. Church buildings may become albatrosses around the collective neck of small congregations. There may be too many of them in a town. Some may be ugly, or represent attitudes to ritual no longer shared by those who gather there. None of these factors denies the basic urge to set a place apart for worship, and the understandable wish to protect and defend it thereafter.

Within a church there is often an area set apart from the bulk of the space, frequently at the eastern end of the church. The Holy Table or Altar is here, and is chiefly used for the principal liturgical act, the sacrament of bread and wine. Sometimes this area is used exclusively by the clergy and their assistants.

The people gathering for worship sit or stand facing the altar part, sometimes with men and women sitting separately, especially in the Orthodox churches.

The clergy often wear robes. In the Orthodox churches these are descended from the garb of the imperial court of Constantinople. In Roman Catholic churches the descent is from the imperial court of Rome. In those churches commonly or loosely called Protestant, the robes are often a combination of the Roman tradition and the dress of a scholar or teacher: a black gown, often with the hood of a university degree. Opinions vary on the importance of liturgical dress.

The Service

Psalms and hymns

Impressive as the continuity of several elements in Christian worship through all the changes of the centuries may be, the continuity of the singing of the psalms from the Hebrew Scriptures is even greater, stretching from centuries before the time of Jesus through the life of the church ever since. What are now called hymns – verses of religious poetry sung to tunes – entered regular church worship mainly during the last one and a half centuries, although some churches have not adopted them at all; but the psalms have been and continue to be sung in the Orthodox churches, in the Roman, Lutheran and Anglican churches, and in churches descending from the Reformed or Presbyterian order. The content of the psalms is varied. Themes of jubilant celebration, penitence and forgiveness, commitment to better behaviour, promises of peace and prosperity and good community life are there, together with pleas for the overthrow of enemies and descriptions of the wickedness of the wicked.

The more recent hymns are often closely related to the psalms and to other parts of the Bible. Like many psalms, they frequently express thoughts and feelings in singular terms ('My God, I love thee') which are sung together by a congregation. They reflect the cultures in which they were written. It has been said that the hymns people sing, or the hymns they like most, can tell you what doctrines or beliefs they have, more accurately than their creeds or official doctrinal statements.

Sin and sins

The note of penitence, remorse and regret is found in the psalms and hymns, and also in prayers said near the beginning of the service. The word prayer is probably most generally taken to mean 'speech addressed to God'. Traditions and individual leaders of worship vary in the sins they think ought to be confessed. Some things would be considered fairly generally to be wrong – telling lies, spreading false disparaging rumours about people, manipulating people and situations to one's own advantage improperly. Other sins of omission might scarcely ruffle respectable consciences – building up fat bank accounts while giving little to people in trouble, for example – and more specifically religious sins, such as not seeking the help of God in time of trouble, would be regarded by non-religious people as not applying to them. It is customary to define sins as wrong actions; but sin has also been understood as separation from God (which to some could be re-expressed as self-centredness). However sin is understood, it is the Christian belief, widely held through the various churches, that God forgives sin – if not automatically, or mechanically – and that the life of Jesus, and especially his death, have much to do with that divine forgiveness. Confession of sin and declaration of forgiveness are important in worship.

The Bible

The reading of passages from the Bible is common in a church service, often with two or three readings (one from the Old Testament and one or two from the New Testament – from the four Gospels and from the other books). The contents of the Bible are considered in a later chapter (Developing the Jewish Heritage). Here I would like to mention two aspects of the reading of the Bible in a church service: the connection between the readings (sometimes called lessons from 'lection', meaning 'reading') and the sermon, and the place of the readings as part of the service in their own right.

In many – probably most – church services today, there is a sermon, or address, or talk, occupying between a quarter and a half of the total length of the service; and in many, or most, instances, the sermon will be connected to the readings. The readings may be laid down for all the churches of that group or denomination, and there are now sets of readings ('lectionaries') agreed internationally and across the denominational lines (so that, for example, a congregation in Edinburgh of the Church of Scotland – which is Presbyterian in order – will hear the same readings that a Roman Catholic congregation in Boston, Massachusetts, USA will hear five hours later). Preachers base what they have to say on how the readings of the day bring out important aspects of Christianity appropriate to the local and wider circumstances of their hearers. The ways in which (A) the meaning of the text, (B) the wider interpretation of the Bible and church teaching, and (C) the personal experience, wisdom, and preference of the preacher are connected in the preparation of the sermon are many and mysterious.

For all the value of relating the lessons to the sermon, it is possible to undervalue the importance of the readings as things to be respected in their own right. Holy books offer more than the sort of meaning that can be employed to urge some better understanding or better conduct on the part of the hearers. The association of words known from child-hood can assist the strengthening and comforting benefit of a sense of continuity and a feeling of belonging, which are important elements in religion. The use of translations from Hebrew and Greek which were made for public reading may have benefit which is less obvious in later translations that did not have that aim of public delivery so central to the translator's work.

The Sermon

I have already made some points about the sermon, and more will be made in the consideration of the Bible, doctrine, and the impact of Christianity on the world around the church. Possibly the sermon is the part of the service which presents least difficulty to anyone who is totally unfamiliar with acts of worship, in that it can be compared to a lecture or an address which might be on any subject, with or without religious connections.

Intercession

It is customary to include reference to people in distress, and to speak about problems and opportunities in the lives of those present – both situations which might exist at any time, such as the care of the environment and the generous reception of strangers, and specific current events, including outbreaks of violence or war, and recent scientific developments calling for judicious and humane response. To some people, intercession involves asking God for help about these matters. For others, questions arise, and are not easily answered, concerning divine power and divine manipulation of human affairs. What all would share is that these prayers involve our thinking about our dangers and opportunities, and doing so within the context of Christian worship.

Baptism

It is the practice of Christian churches, with very few exceptions, to welcome people into the church by baptism, using water. In most churches baptism is given to people of any age, including newborn babies. In Baptist churches baptism is confined to those who make profession of the faith themselves. There are two customary forms of baptism: the pouring of water on the person's head, and the immer-sion of the person completely in water. Baptism is administered sometimes in separate services and sometimes at regular Sunday services.

The Eucharist

It is probably the case that in most Sunday morning services in churches throughout the world the chief place and high point is the sacrament involving bread and wine, when communicants receive either the bread only, or the bread and the wine. This is the heart of Christian worship and requires separate treatment.

Blessing

The service usually ends with the leader (priest, minister) blessing the people in the name of God, as they are encouraged to go out and live their lives in harmony with the perspective and assumptions of their worship.

A church service in a Christian church will have much in common with similar events of other religions. It will also reflect the place and time in which it happens. Central to every service will be the significance accorded to Jesus Christ.

Approaching Understanding:
The Apostles' Creed

Involvement in Christianity is both individual and communal. At times the individual element has become swamped by the common factor, the swamping being particularly effective when the communally shared aspects of involvement are more imposed by some authority than accepted freely by the group or community. Christian involvement is also both a matter of thought and a matter of practice. Contemporary culture in the West tends to emphasise individual choice over common conviction, and religion as the holding of opinions over religion as the activity of worship. The matter might be expressed by the contrasting terms 'I think' and 'We do'. The point I am making is that involvement in the Christian religion is both 'what I think' and 'what we do'; and that the second aspect, 'what we do', emphasising the communal and the practical, calls for special commendation in the modern western world. ('What we think' and 'what I do' are also present, of course.)

From that point of departure I would like to visit the Apostles' Creed, that ancient agreed summary of Christian believing, and offer some comments and ask some questions to give some help, I hope, on the journey towards greater understanding of Christianity.

I believe in God the Father Almighty, Maker of Heaven and Earth

The word 'God' is, I think, for many people the, or a chief barrier to, further consideration of the Christian religion. I do not know what moves are made in the mind to erect this barrier; but if they include an assumption that believers have a sort of picture of God in their minds, and that this picture corresponds to the reality of someone like that being there, somewhere, I have to say that I do not have any such picture, and I do not think there is any backing in the Bible for the holding of such a picture. 'God' was not a word upon which to speculate philosophically in the Hebrew Scriptures. It is a word for using in practical situations rather than a concept employed in building a theory of how everything fits together. Offering thanks for all that is good, crying out in pain about things that are wrong, longing for better days and seeking help in bringing them to pass – 'God' is used then, to indicate the comprehensive nature of the reference, and the personal relationship one has with it. 'God' is a very unusual word. It is not a proper name, like Napoleon or Nairobi. It is more of an expressive, practical term, indicating a fundamental, ultimate dimension of life.

When we say we 'believe in' God the Father Almighty, Maker of Heaven and Earth, we are expressing a hopeful trust that focuses our deepest, truest, best values in a perspective which is both personal and relates to all that is – Heaven and Earth, things measurable and things immeasurable, the physical world and the spiritual dimension.

It is when we come to the next part of the creed that we may, possibly, come nearer to the notion of pictorial imagery of the divine.

And in Jesus Christ, his only Son our Lord, who was conceived by the Holy Ghost, born of the Virgin Mary, suffered under Pontius Pilate, was crucified, dead, and buried

The modern interest in finding out more and more of the details of the lives of prominent people, whether distinguished or notorious, was scarcely present in the ancient world. Details were not recorded as in our world. Also, legends and myths were readily composed to indicate the significance of the great ones, and it was more important that the impact or 'truth' of the person be communicated than that the story have factual accuracy, as is expected of, say, a police report. Even when the four Gospels about Jesus were written they had little in common with biographies, while the earlier letters of Paul show little interest by the great missionary Apostle in Jesus' teaching and relationship with people, and even less in his appearance and the bits and pieces of his daily living which would be required in a modern biography. So the creed moves directly from Jesus' birth to his trial and death sentence from Pontius Pilate. If we continue to regard believing as practice more than theory, we may ask how the things said about Jesus are incorporated into our worship, and thus reflect our values.

To say that Jesus was God's only son is not to make a claim to biological ancestry as much as it is a claim that the character of Jesus is, for Christian people, a deeply significant element in that focus on the ultimate, fundamental dimension which is the core of worship. Today that 'colouring in' of the heart of life would probably involve what we might regard as the attractive goodness of Jesus, the teaching we like best, and, for some more than others, his works of wonder. For Paul and many of the framers of the early agreed statements of essential Christianity, the specific character and conduct of Jesus seemed much less important than the fact that his being alive and his death on the cross were a link between God and people, a means of reconciling earth to heaven, the human with the divine. Doubtless it is inevitable that different aspects of the impact of Jesus have caught people's attention at different times, and we should probably not be greatly concerned that it has, in practice, meant more than one thing among Christian people to speak of Jesus as God's son. What matters more is that the significant things about Jesus inform and colour our sense of our deepest values, and therefore what we cherish in worship and behaviour.

He descended into hell. The third day he rose again from the dead, he ascended into heaven, and sitteth on the right hand of God the Father Almighty; from thence he shall come to judge the quick and the dead

Here is more affirmation of the ultimate significance of Jesus, or, if you prefer, of the way in which people have been able to regard his life as a lens through which to see great mysteries, a specific through which things general and universal may be known, or spoken of. The life of Christ is a mirror, in which the universal providence of God, everywhere at work, is reflected to those who are called by his name.

I believe in the Holy Ghost; the Holy Catholic Church; the Communion of Saints; the Forgiveness of Sins; the Resurrection of the Body; and the Life Everlasting.

An attempt will be made to say something about this list later. For the present, it may be worth making the point that faith, or belief, or religious involvement is shared, and held together, as well as being held by the individual believer. When the detailed list of things in the creeds brings about a tightening of the lips, as mental scruples stand in the way of giving audible agreement to one line or another, it can be helpful to bear in mind that the same lips have opened wide to sing lines of hymns which appear to commit the singer to far more detailed agreement than the line in the creed on the same subject which the singer was unable to articulate. The assumption may be that hymns are different, in being communal, and not exactly statements of agreement. I maintain that lines in creeds are like lines in hymns, or at least much more like them than may often be supposed. A distinguished theologian once said 'I can no longer say the creed, but I can sing it.' My point is that, in that case, he should have been able to say it.

Faith, it seems to me, is not so much the holding of opinions on religious matters as it is the inhabiting of an environment of nourishing imagery. The nature of that environment will be varied, and the ingredients which seem prominent will change from time to time. For Christian people, Jesus Christ will be central, but the aspects and interpretations of him will appear to change. It will tend to be significant that shared faith exists, both with contemporaries and in a happy dependence on predecessors; that signs and reminders are present of renewal and forgiveness; of this life being in continuity with things yet to come; of there always being scope for mysterious new beginnings, creative connections, ladders between earth and heaven – things of the Spirit.

The Apostles' Creed is not the private judgement of one, but the expression of a common perspective, shared variously by varied individuals.

One Man's Life

There is an old story about a Scottish poet who composed a song in honour of his wife, Mary, celebrating her youthful beauty in lavish, generous terms. One day two travellers came by the poet's cottage. They had heard the song, and they wished to see for themselves this person of outstanding beauty. They were invited into the house, and emerged soon after, with disappointment written on their faces. 'Is that the fair young Mary?' 'Ah,' said the poet, 'you did not see her with my eyes.' It is, perhaps, a simple little tale. It makes the point, however, that perception in the perspective of devotion is different from perception in the spirit of disinterested scientific enquiry. Very little is known about Jesus from the latter standpoint, although it is possible to make a short historical statement about him. Most of what was written about him in the half-century after his death was written by people to whom he had become powerfully important. They saw him through eyes of devotion. The books of the Bible which have some appearance of biographies of Jesus (Matthew, Mark, Luke and John) were written not so much to give objective data as to proclaim a cause. Out of their practice of faith they were commending the same practice to others. Religion, as I have already said, is more a matter of what we do than of what I think.

When I say that the four books of Matthew, Mark, Luke and John (the first four books that you come to in the New Testament, but not the first to be written – and more of that later) appear to have some of the features of biographical writings about Jesus, there is no suggestion that they are bad biographies, or failed, or inadequate 'lives' of Jesus. You might criticise a modern biography of some recent figure for omitting any reference to his childhood, ignoring whole decades of his life, telling you nothing of his physical appearance, and providing you with little understanding of his close and intimate relationships with men and women; but such omissions are largely what Matthew, Mark, Luke and John share, though without any note of failure – since that sort of biography is not at all what they were attempting to write. Two of the four make no reference to Jesus' birth, and the other two write about it in a way which suggests that religious points are being made through the telling of a sequence of events, the underlying point being of much greater significance than the factual accuracy of the narrative. Only one of the four refers to any event in his youth; and all four seem to devote virtually all their space to the last three years of his life, when he was about thirty. We do not even know if he was married. A distinguished scholar of the cultural environment of Jesus' time told me that it was so unusual for a man of thirty never to have been married that it is more surprising that his bachelor status is not mentioned: the conclusion which the scholar reached being that Jesus was more likely to have been a widower than a bachelor.

I recognise that the point about Jesus' marital status may annoy and offend some devout Christian people. I include it in a book about the search for an understanding of Christianity, however, because I think that one factor to be faced in such a search is the assumption that in Christian believing clear and detailed knowledge or conviction will always be present, on quite a number of matters, about God and Jesus, and spiritual, doctrinal, and moral implications of the faith. There are, indeed, many things which many Christian people have in common, and there are also statements – creeds – which serve as points of reference by which to assess the exploration of individual minds. But to many people it will not be helpful to suggest that spiritual insight can be equated with detailed opinions on matters about which they feel such precision is inappropriate, and indeed impossible. Their attitude may be said to be vindicated by the openness of the earliest reports about Jesus – his sayings and his doings – leaving a great deal to the readers and hearers to interpret and re-express in changing times and cultures. Into that openness we can happily place our lack of knowledge about the historical details of the life of Jesus. If people have an idea in their minds of the physical appearance of Jesus, that picture will owe much to religious art, probably from fifteen hundred years or so after his life. If they feel they know the sort of person he was, in disposition and facets of personality, such an identikit photograph is likely to come through cultural filters and not at all to be the only possible 'picture' of the man they can have – if, indeed, having that sort of picture is necessary or helpful to Christian faith. If they assume that the life of Jesus has certain clear and indisputable implications for what to believe about him, what to believe about God, and what to believe about personal and social behaviour, it would be good if they paused and considered the great possibility that fresh or recovered insight is always possible (and that respectable institutions like the Church tend to impose order on creative disturbance, and try to make the wild elements tame).

In order to suspect that our notion of the character of Jesus may be too respectable, too tame, too much the product of the culture of some of his well-intentioned followers, we may consider that the unique voice of heaven to earth is unlikely to fit our assumptions like a glove. But it is not necessary to make so grand a claim. It would be enough to bear in mind, with a recent writer, that 'Jesus was a Jew living in a culture different from our own, with presuppositions that may appear to us jarring.' [J. C. Paget in *Cambridge Companion to Jesus* (Cambridge University Press, 2001), p. 2.]

When did Jesus live? It was more than five hundred years after the birth of Jesus that the practice came into being of counting the years from the year in which it was believed he had been born. Each year was regarded as a year in which he was the Lord (AD = Anno Domini = in the year of the Lord). For a century and more, however, it has been widely accepted that the estimated year of his birth was wrong, and that, odd as it seems, he was probably born around 6 BC (that is, six years before Christ, or six years before the beginning of the period when the years were referred to as AD). It is likely that he died around AD 30 – 33 (or CE – in the Common Era – as dates are now sometimes given).

Where did he live? He lived in Galilee, and spent time also in Judaea, especially in the town of Jerusalem. Galilee and Judaea were part of the Roman Empire, which came into being only twenty-five years before Jesus' birth. They were also the land of the Hebrew people, the Jews, and had been for more than a thousand years. These two elements, the Hebrew background and the Roman Empire, were both central to the formation and development of Christianity. A glance at the Bible, the greater part of which is the Old Testament (or Hebrew Bible), will convey something of the fundamental significance of its Jewish roots to the Christian religion. The importance of the Roman Empire, seen in many ways, may be suggested by the fact that the first emperor, Augustus, great nephew of Julius Caesar, presided over the settlement of the old republic into an empire lasting 500 years, the first 200 of which were years of peace and prosperity, with a uniform legal system, ease of travel, and a supporting army, while also including much diversity of local custom and religious practice. The combination of unity and diversity held also for language, with local languages co-existing with two imperial languages, Latin in the west and Greek in the east. In Jesus' time the empire surrounded the Mediterranean and reached the north of France. Later, it included Britain and eastern Europe, as well as stretching farther into Asia to encompass Mesopotamia, the land of the Tigris and the Euphrates, home to some of earth's most ancient habitations. It is no accident that the name Jesus is a Greek version of the Hebrew Joshua. (The New Testament was written in Greek. The Old Testament, the Hebrew Bible, was written, unsurprisingly, in Hebrew.)

According to the first chapters of Matthew and Luke, Jesus was born in Bethlehem, a town in Judaea near Jerusalem, and associated with King David, the Jewish people's most cherished king, who lived in the tenth century before Jesus (BC). That is possible, though some scholars now think it more likely that he was born in Nazareth, where he grew up, and that these writers located his birth in Bethlehem in order to make, or emphasise, a connection between him and the great David. His parents were Joseph and Mary, though Matthew and Luke attribute his conception to God acting directly, and to no human biological father being involved. They both give long ancestral lines to Jesus, through Joseph not Mary, and so Joseph must have had some significance for them. Opinions vary among Christian people as to whether the claim of the Virgin Birth is to be taken as fact, or as poetic and symbolic; and among those who accept it as part of the Christian tradition, some will be more devoted than others to defending it as significant for authentic Christian faith.

Although the duration of Jesus' 'public' life is not given in the Bible, it appears to have lasted about three years (the calculation, or guess, being made from studying the accounts of his doings in the four Gospels – Matthew, Mark, Luke and, especially for this purpose, John). His public activities included speaking to large groups of hearers but also, and perhaps more often, to a smaller group of followers or disciples. These disciples were probably not confined to the twelve, though they were central, and probably included women. This time was also marked by his exercise of special powers of healing and over nature. His sayings, as remembered, largely avoided abstract philosophising or doctrinal argument, and concentrated on parables, stories about everyday happenings and pointed, humorous remarks. Is it possible to have some imaginative picture in our heads of the atmosphere of the times spent by Jesus and his group in and around the fishing village of Capernaum, on the Sea of Galilee (or Lake of Tiberias, as it is also known)? When you remember that 1,900 million people (according to a 1999 estimate) profess some allegiance to the man, it would be absurd to try to prevent them from having some picture in their minds of what he was like. It might also be thought to fit badly with the concrete down-to-earth character of his talk if he were to be remembered more in ideas and general principles than in living flesh and blood. But we have to accept that much of the colouring of our Jesus-picture will come from our own preferences and needs – from how we would like him to have been. Other colouring will come from seeing that part of the world as it is today – directly or in photographs – though for many that is not required. For them, the scenery of Galilee can be replaced by the landscape that they know, and a Palestinian face replaced by an African or Oriental one. Walk into an Italian art gallery or church, and there you will see pictures of Jesus looking like a young Italian man, in scenes set in the landscape of Tuscany or Umbria or Le Marche. Thus is a sense of the universal significance of Jesus set forth in art.

This mixing of historical investigation and pious reconstruction can lead not only to a detailed colouring-in of the aspects of Jesus' life which we do not know, but also to a sense that, though we know little, there is enough to influence our lives deeply. Albert Schweitzer's *Quest of the Historical Jesus* (London, A & C Black, 1911, p. 3) contains lines that have become widely known and frequently quoted:

> He comes to us as One unknown, without a name, as of old, by the lakeside, He came to those men who knew Him not. He speaks to us the same word: 'Follow thou me!', and sets us to the tasks which He has to fulfil for our time. He commands. And to those who obey Him, whether they be wise or simple, He will reveal Himself in the toils, the conflicts, the sufferings which they shall pass through in His fellowship, and, as an ineffable mystery, they shall learn in their own experience Who He is.

But we do know his name. Or do we? Jesus, yes, but what about Christ? The Roman writer Tacitus, who lived in the first and second centuries of the Christian era, wrote about *Christus* (in Latin) as Jesus' name; but *khristos* is a Greek word meaning 'anointed', the translation of a Hebrew word which also means the same, and which in English is the word messiah. Jesus Christ therefore means Jesus the Anointed. People were anointed (that is, oil was poured on them) to indicate selection for and appointment to an office or position of some importance. Kings, especially, were anointed. It happens still for British sovereigns at their coronation. To call Jesus the Christ meant that you regarded him as chosen for a great purpose. It also meant that you believed that the purpose was one which had featured in the visionary writings of Hebrew prophets who foresaw the special activity of God at some future time. Jesus was believed by his followers to be Christ – THAT Christ.

Possibly the one thing which most people know about Jesus is that he was crucified – that is, he was killed by crucifixion. It happened in Jerusalem. We shall consider later the significance of the events surrounding his death, the most important of them being the Last Supper and the Resurrection. For the present, we might revisit the possibility that the man was wilder than might be suggested by some elements of his image as promoted by the churches. Would a tame man have provoked the wrath of established, respectable authority? How subversive was he of settled government and civilised ways? Such questions will return as we try to understand not only the man who became known as the Christ, but also those who have professed to follow him, and to represent him, through nearly two thousand years.

Developing the Jewish Heritage

The impact which Jesus made on his followers was so great that some of them have always tended to play down the dependence of Christianity on its Jewish past. Possibly they may not have tried deliberately to underestimate its significance; rather they have wished to proclaim and celebrate the special qualities of Jesus as they saw them, and in doing so they have emphasised a perceived uniqueness which may have left his Jewish roots unspoken or even rejected. The fact, however, that the Hebrew holy book (which the church has called the Old Testament) occupies fully three-quarters of the Christian holy book (the Bible) confirms the official Christian view that Jesus' Jewish roots are of profound and irreplaceable importance in the formation of Christian thinking, beginning with, and including, the teaching of Jesus as recorded in the New Testament (that is, the Christian quarter of the Bible).

It may give some perspective to the understanding of Christianity and its Jewish roots to bear in mind that the Old Testament covers approximately a period of two thousand years – that is, about the same length of time for which Christianity has existed. It should, however, be emphasised immediately that the pages of the Old Testament are not devoted proportionately to these two thousand years (any more than the four Gospels are devoted in equal number of pages per year to each of the thirty-three years of Jesus' life). Much of the writing (or editing, or compiling) of the books of the Old Testament was done in the eighth, seventh, and sixth centuries BC, and can be summarised as follows.

The First Five Books

The first five books of the Bible – Genesis, Exodus, Leviticus, Numbers, and Deuteronomy – bring together written and oral tradition covering what had happened in Hebrew history and heritage prior to the settlement in the 'promised land' (roughly present day Israel/Palestine) shortly before 1000 BC. These five books are the fundamental authority for Judaism, taking precedence over the rest of the Hebrew Scriptures, and represent the basic section of the holy book for Jewish people. They include poetic, mythical tales about the creation of the world, stories about the nomadic patriarchs of c. 2000 –

1800 BC, and, most importantly, the emancipation of their people from Egypt under the leadership of Moses. That liberation, the exodus, provided a memory and defining symbol of who the Hebrew people were, and its significance has been carried into the imagery of Christian people, chiefly through the significance of the Eucharist but also by identifying people without freedom with the enslaved Hebrews in Egypt (as in the spiritual, 'Go down Moses, way down in Egypt's land, and tell old Pharaoh, Let my people go', sung by plantation slaves in the southern American states).

History Books

The books of Joshua, Judges, Samuel, Kings, Chronicles, Ezra and Nehemiah 'cover' the period from the death of Moses (perhaps around 1250 BC until the fifth century BC). They are not like modern history books. Some parts are direct accounts of what happened there and then – notably at the court of King Solomon – while others bring together long-remembered tales well worked through the evolution of oral tradition. The reign of Solomon was a time of peace and prosperity unmatched by any later period. Solomon's father David (Israel's second king) provided the platform for his son's success, by unifying the people and establishing Jerusalem as their capital, the centre of government and the nation's religious shrine. Solomon took advant-age of the trade routes passing through his land, and derived wealth from the mining of copper and tin. He built a temple, which became the religious centre for all the people, as it remained, in rebuilt form, at the time of Jesus. After Solomon things quickly began to go wrong. His sons fought one another, and the country was divided into two: a northern kingdom of Israel centred on Samaria, and a southern kingdom, Judah, whose capital was Jerusalem. Both kingdoms were prey to successive invading armies, and the northern kingdom collapsed in the eighth century BC. One particular defeat of the southern kingdom was of deep and lasting significance, when the Babylonians took Jerusalem and carried away a significant proportion of the people into exile in Babylon. After 587 BC, that exile lasted fifty years until the Babylonians were conquered by the Persians. It was an episode of spiritual growth and insight, and left an indelible mark on the developing understanding of God and his ways.

The Prophets

There are fifteen books bearing the names of individuals who are collectively called prophets: three large books, of Isaiah, Jeremiah and Ezekiel, and twelve much shorter books (Isaiah is divisible into three parts, each written by a different author). For much of

Christian history these books were prized partly or largely because they were believed to contain predictions of future events which were fulfilled through the life and impact of Jesus. For the past century or so, however, scholars of the Christian traditions have regarded the prophets much more as men with a message for their own times. It is not difficult to find instances of such proclamations in which the judgement of their God is declared by the prophet, namely as an announcement that the people are behaving badly:

> These are the words of the Lord of Hosts the God of Israel: Amend your ways and your deeds, that I may let you live in this place. You keep saying, 'this place is the temple of the Lord, the temple of the Lord, the temple of the Lord!' This slogan of yours is a lie; put not trust in it. If you amend your ways and your deeds, deal fairly with one another, cease to oppress the alien, the fatherless, and the widow, if you shed no innocent blood in this place and do not run after other gods to your own ruin, then I shall let you live in this place, in the land which long ago I gave to your forefathers for all time.
> (Jeremiah 7: 3-7)

The clear conviction of the prophet that he knows the mind of God, the insistence that religious activity must be accompanied by neighbourly citizenship, the recollection of a destiny declared long ago, and the linking of right behaviour to inhabiting the land are regular marks of prophetic writing. Sometimes the judgement is declared without a message of restoration, but the note of the rescuing God is often present. In the second part of Isaiah there are passages concerning a 'servant' of God, which have been seen as strongly foretelling the story of the death of Jesus and its significance centuries beforehand. There was undoubtedly an idea in the mind of the writer that one person – or possibly one group, or even race – could suffer 'for' others. The fifty-third chapter of the book called Isaiah so powerfully expresses what many Christian people have felt and believed about the suffering and death of Jesus, although the words were written, probably, five hundred years or so earlier. The thought also comes to mind that Jesus' conduct was affected by Isaiah's words – or that the writers of the New Testament, in giving an account of Jesus' death, and in exploring its deep meaning, employed Isaiah's imagery to put into words something they could not find better words to describe.

> He was wounded for our transgressions, he was bruised for our iniquities: the chastisement of our peace was upon him; and with his stripes we are healed. (Isaiah 53: 5)

The Psalms and Other Poetry

Other books in the Old Testament include some which cannot easily be classified, such as Esther, Ruth, Daniel, and the poetical books, Song of Solomon, Ecclesiastes, Proverbs, Job, Lamentations, each of which contains beauty and insight. The Psalms, however, stand out, as the songbook not only of the Jewish people but of the Christian church. A twentieth-century scholar, G.W. Anderson, has written that while 'the prophetic literature records the message of exceptional men, in the Psalter we have the poems in which the worship and devotion of the ordinary man were expressed.' For many parts of the church, singing has been more or less confined, until the past two centuries, to words from the Bible (that is, excluding hymns or religious songs composed in more recent times). Apart from some songs from the New Testament, it meant that the Old Testament Psalms were – and are – used to express differing moods of people at their worship: celebration and thanksgiving, sadness and lament, dedication to live good lives, and more.

> O be joyful in the Lord, all ye lands! (Psalm 100: 1)

> Praise the Lord from the earth, ye dragons, and all deeps: fire and hail; snow and vapour; stormy wind fulfilling his word! (Psalm 148: 7-8)

> Turn us again, O God, and cause thy face to shine; and we shall be saved.
> O Lord of hosts, how long wilt thou be angry against the prayer of thy people?
> Thou feedest them with the bread of tears; and givest them tears to drink in great measure. (Psalm 80: 4-5)

> What man is he that desireth life, and loveth many days, that he may see good?
> Keep thy tongue from evil, and thy lips from speaking guile.
> Depart from evil, and do good; seek peace, and pursue it. (Psalm 34: 12-14)

The Covenant and the Ten Commandments

There is a sense of destiny which leads to a will to change things, to participate in the making of a better future. The patriarch Abraham, a biblical figure emerging from the time before history, represents the risky journey of faith. He is portrayed as being called by God to leave his homeland and travel to a new place of which he knew nothing, with the promise that 'in thee and in thy seed shall all the families of the earth be blessed'. That ancient notion stayed with the Hebrew people, though at times it was eclipsed: the notion that they had a vocation to be of service to the whole world, that their destiny was not to succeed at the expense of their neighbours, but to serve their neighbours. It is not surprising that the idea was sometimes ignored. Defence of national interests in the twenty-first century, the assumption that our loyalty is to our country 'right or wrong', makes the notion that the whole earth is our homeland remain an idea whose hour often seems still some time away.

The idea of morality being both social and demonstrably for people's good is one which lies deep in the Hebrew heritage. Loving neighbours, caring for the unfortunate, making special provision for the poor, the aliens, the neglected – such generosity is built into the precepts put forward in the first five books of the Bible.

There is also a clear connection between religious ritual and social responsibility. It was not enough to fulfil your religious duty. The service of God and the service of neighbour were inseparable.

The idea of a covenant between God and people is central to the Jewish legacy. Under the leadership of Moses, as they journeyed from Egyptian slavery to the promised land, the people entered into an agreement of trust, whereby they understood God to be committing himself to be faithful to them, as they committed themselves to be faithful to God. The preface to the Ten Commandments, that best-known of guides to the right way to live, emphasises the liberation they had received as the basis of their following these precepts.

> I am the Lord your God who brought you out of Egypt, out of the land of slavery. (Exodus 20: 2)

The basis of God's trustworthiness was not his divine authority, or his superior power, but their past experience of the liberation which they had received through his action.

It is of interest to observe that the Ten Commandments are just that, ten in number. The first three have to do with God and how to regard him; the fourth concerns the keeping of the Sabbath day; the fifth requires the honouring of parents. Then there follow the prohibitions of murder, adultery, theft, lying, and covetousness. People sometimes say they think we should return to these Ten Commandments. Do they appreciate that no distinction is made in the list, say between the important commandments and the ones it is all right to ignore? To extract numbers six to nine, or even these plus number five, possibly adding the tenth, while omitting, for practical purposes, the first four, is to remove the code from the context which is its life blood, and to forget the significance of those events, rituals, and gestures in any company which testify to its deepest values and keep them fresh and potent. We may not choose to keep the Sabbath in the particular ways in which some of our predecessors kept it; but society needs patterns, and patterns need symbols, common gestures, festivals.

As for not worshipping idols, perhaps we need in the modern world to learn that whatever else worship of God may mean, it can be a deeply liberating implication of such a devotion to hold that nothing else is to be worshipped, that no convention or country requires that we sell our souls to serve them.

There is always a risk in reducing the rich heritage of a living culture to a few summarised conclusions; but the possibility of such summarising tending to rob the colourful diversity of the Old Testament of its life should not prevent us claiming and stating that the Jewish background to Christianity is always in danger of underestimation, for it is very great in value.

Among so much else that the Old Testament gives us, it valuably gives no one specified description of God. There is more of the aural image of one who speaks than of any visual image of dimension or old-man-in-the-sky anthropomorphism. It is helpful to the Christian development that no picture or image of God is prescribed.

But how rich and varied are the pictures, the stories, the ideas we receive in these old sacred writings which we share with Jewish friends – the Garden of Eden, Noah's Ark, the Tower of Babel, Abraham and Isaac, Joseph and his brothers, the Burning Bush, bricks without straw, the Golden Calf, Water from the Rock, David and Goliath, Solomon and the Queen of Sheba, and so much more. It is the record of a people's journey, not reduced into abstract generalities or sanitised into safe precepts, but messy and violent, with intrigue and cunning, with friendship and love and longing. Great poetry is there, and great insight, with the unsystematic mixture of life. All that lies behind Jesus and Christianity.

The Cross of the Risen Christ

How is the Christian religion to be presented to an interested enquirer? Such a person can easily be imagined saying 'Give me the facts. I will decide what my reaction is once I know the facts.' Can such an attitude be applied to the beginnings of Christianity? Much will depend on what our interested enquirer is prepared to accept as facts. If for example, she says tell me about the life of Jesus, without the loaded account of that life which a devoted follower might give, we would have to reply that that is just not possible. Only through the perspective of discipleship are we told about Jesus. If she goes on to insist that talk of his resurrection is too much for her; but she would like to give a fair consideration to the significance of Jesus while leaving aside the matter of his resurrection; then we would need to tell her that what she is asking for is an unchristian account of Christ – a response to Jesus which ignores or denies that central claim without which the world would in all probability never have heard of the man. The appeal of the exhortation to love your enemies, and the insistence on the importance of children, and of foreigners (such as Samaritans) may be very great. But these sayings from the life of Jesus in Galilee would never have reached us if a group of people had not been filled with the desire to tell the world about the one whom they called their Lord, once put to death on a cross, then raised to life and somehow with them still.

Given that focus of conviction, it would not be surprising if it struck a clear-sighted observer as rather odd that the one universally recognised symbol of the Christian religion is derived from the two pieces of wood on which he was hanged until he died. It is true that in some church traditions, notably of the Orthodox world, Jesus is presented in shining gold as glorious and divine, with symbols of majesty and power. For much of organised Christianity, however, the cross is the chief emblem of the faith. Thousands have gathered with shouts of celebration and thanksgiving in acts of worship where the visual symbol at the centre is the man on the cross. Good reasons may be given for the practice. What would be worthy of comment is any evident lack of bemusement at taking the instrument of weakness and condemnation and death to be the focus of adoration and cheerful rejoicing (as well as of other moods of worship).

It is true that no period in Jesus' life was recorded with such concern for detail as the day before and the day of his crucifixion, from the Last Supper with the disciples until his burial. Two qualifications must be made, however, to the statement that Matthew, Mark, Luke and John *recorded* the events leading up to and including Jesus' crucifixion. One is that these writers were not journalists seeking to provide a graphic account of the events with plenty of local colour and illuminating quotations from bystanders and leading players. They were concerned with the significance of the betrayal, arrest, trials and crucifixion as events that supported their main convictions about Jesus, and the ways in which the Hebrew Scriptures provided backing to their interpretation. (Just read Psalm 22.) The other thing to be said is that there is nothing of tear-jerking sentimentality in what is written. Jesus is not described in a way that is calculated to develop pity for him. His feelings are scarcely mentioned. In John's account the opposite of weakness and misery is suggested: royal and divine authority and confidence mark John's Jesus as he makes his way to his cross. That may give some clue to the choice of the cross as the Christian symbol.

It might also be noted that the gibbet on which Jesus and many others were executed was shaped more like the letter T than the usual cross-shape, which is a + with the vertical line extended. Some have suggested that such a sign is older than Christianity and is a symbol to which people are drawn, quite independently of its Christian association. That could be a comforting thought to those who see the Christian religion as naturally suited to human circumstances, while to others it may be an irrelevant coincidence. It ought to be said that it is perfectly possible to hold the view that Christianity is well suited to human nature without denying that other religions are also so suited. Jesus is quoted as saying two things which appear to go in opposite directions, 'The person who is not with us is against us', and 'those who are not against us are on our side'. The first suggests an exclusive attitude, the second a more inclusive one. The first is probably quoted more frequently, and that may be because people of exclusive minds may tend to be more dominant, more vociferous in religion, whereas those of a more inclusive perspective may be more likely to be quiet, tolerant, and passive. There may be something of a built-in contradiction in being an enthusiastic liberal, even when one is convinced that open-minded, non-judgemental tolerance is authentically Christian and true to the spirit of Jesus.

What is not in doubt is the central claim among the first members of the church that Jesus 'died and rose again', as Paul puts it in the earliest piece of writing in the New Testament, his First Letter (or Epistle) to the Thessalonians (1 Thessalonians 4: 14). So essential was the conviction, that he could write, in his First Letter to the Corinthians, 'if Christ was not raised, then our gospel is null and void, and so too is your faith' (1 Corinthians 15: 17).

Paul, the first great missionary and interpreter of Christianity, wrote his epistles before the Gospels were written, and all – epistles and Gospels – can be dated to the fifty years from AD 50 to 100 (or very near). Paul writes of Jesus appearing to believers after his death (including over five hundred at one time); but it is not claimed that he ever appeared to unbelievers, or observers. Paul includes himself 'last of all' in the list of those to whom Jesus appeared. The description of Paul's conversion on the road to Damascus (Acts 9) tells of a bright light that blinded him and the voice of Jesus that spoke – but nobody saw the speaker. The four Gospels tell the story of Jesus' burial tomb being found empty, with differing details, all agreeing both that the tomb was empty and that it was found empty by Mary Magdalene and possibly one or more other women. The earliest version of Mark has a young man telling the women that Jesus was risen. In Matthew, two women are met by an angel, and then by Jesus himself, who also appears to disciples in Galilee. Luke tells a fuller tale, both in the book which bears his name and in the Acts of the Apostles (which describes the growth of the church, chiefly through Paul's missionary work). Luke tells of two angels meeting the women at the tomb, Peter then going to the tomb, and two disciples walking with Jesus but not recognising him until a meal begins (and he vanishes). Peter sees him, the company of disciples then see him suddenly appear, he eats with them, and later he commissions them and blesses them and 'while he blessed them, he was parted from them, and carried up into heaven' (Luke 24: 51). In Acts, Luke says that Jesus was forty days with the disciples, or that he made appearances in that period, after which he was taken up. John tells of Mary confusing the risen Jesus with the gardener, of Thomas being urged by Jesus to touch him to know that his presence is physical, and (in an appended chapter) of Jesus offering a meal by the Sea of Galilee and commissioning Peter to leadership in the church. There is nothing particularly strange in varied accounts reaching the second-generation Christian compilers of the Gospels. Whatever the experience was, it was of such significance and surprise, and so incapable of fitting into regular categories of description, that different elements inevitably were preserved by different individuals, groups, or 'chains of memory'.

Should we call the resurrection surprising, when the Gospels have predictions of it recorded as being made long beforehand? The Gospels were written backward, from the resurrection as the motive for publishing the story of Jesus, through the events which had gone before. Jesus may have spoken of his rising; but that scarcely removes the element of confused astonishment among the disciples on Easter morning. As for 'regular categories' with which to express in concepts and words the mysterious 'rising' of Jesus, such things are probably more puzzling to modern people than to Palestinian Jews of the first century; and even if 'resurrection' was a concept with some meaning in Jewish culture, it is unlikely to have been without difficulty. It is also the case that, by the time the Gospels were written (indeed the reason for their being written), Christian groups were in existence with little or no Jewish elements or background.

What did they think the resurrection was? Was it a question they asked? It was certainly a way in which they could go on to speak first of Jesus who was crucified, and then of Jesus Christ the Lord in glory 'seated at the right hand of the Father', and of one person bearing these two descriptions. Possibly for many Christian believers, then and ever since, that is enough, and no further questions need be asked. For those who may be uncomfortable with the thought that they are being asked to believe the impossible, three points might be made. The first is that nowhere in the New Testament is any attempt made to describe the resurrection as an event – that his heart started beating again, or that the process of bodily decay was reversed at some moment early on Easter Sunday morning. Second, the Jesus who appeared in the gospel accounts is significantly different from the Jesus who was crucified, in that disciples at times did not recognise him, and also he was able to appear and disappear through locked doors (while confusingly not being a ghost, as well as being able to eat fish, and be touched by Thomas). We are not free to conclude that the resurrection was the restoration of Jesus, who again became exactly what he had been before his death. It is unhelpful to stretch people's credulity by presenting the resurrection as a miracle of resuscitation. The third, and more general, point is that there is a good deal of imagery and metaphor in such things as 'ascended into heaven' and 'seated at the right hand'. Although the word 'resurrection' now has the feel of a technical term, the word comes from the Latin *surgere*, to rise, and thus it also is being used in a way not unlike the use of 'ascent' or even 'he came down to earth from heaven'. It is not that these claims are untrue; but they are not the sort of event you might have photographed.

There is about the New Testament writings such a measure of diversity that the succeeding church's efforts to make a coherent system of the rudiments of Christianity were probably inevitable. Also the reading and studying of these writings at the meetings for worship throughout the centuries have exposed the New Testament books and the minds of the hearers to each other, thus allowing the unsystematised memories of Jesus to make their impact on generations of Christian people and encourage fresh insight and interpretation in the different environments of the church through the ages. Luke alone, for example, tells of the news of Jesus' birth coming to shepherds from an angelic messenger. He alone gives three songs which have been part of the church's continuing worship: the Benedictus, the song of John the Baptist's father; the Magnificat, the song of Jesus' mother, Mary; and the Nunc Dimittis, the song of Simeon in the temple. Only Luke gives us two of the most loved stories or parables attributed to Jesus, the Good Samaritan and the Prodigal Son. Only he gives the 40/50 chronology in which Jesus' resurrection was followed forty days later by his ascension, which was followed ten days after that by the inspiration of the disciples at Pentecost; Pentecost was the Jewish festival held fifty days after Passover, which in turn commemorated the exodus from Egypt under Moses. Pentecost means 'fiftieth' in Greek.

From Synagogue to Church

The word synagogue is the English version of a Greek word which means 'coming together', and is thus the Greek equivalent of the word congregation. The English word church comes, through some intermediary words, from the Greek adjective *kuriakos* meaning 'of the Lord'. The Lord is Jesus, who was known at an early stage of Christianity as both Christ (the anointed one, or Messiah) and Lord. Synagogues were meeting places of Jewish people, but the word was also used for several centuries to refer to the meeting place of the followers of Jesus. In the first century groups of Jewish people were to be found in cities of the Roman Empire around the Mediterranean, including Rome itself, and these synagogues attracted non-Jewish people who were not willing to become Jews, but found elements of the worship, doctrine and morality of the Jewish people attractive. These people, known as 'God-fearers', were often among the first to join the new Christian communities, and their presence is one of the reasons for the spread of the new faith in Jesus within decades of his death. By AD 64, a little over thirty years after the crucifixion, there were enough Christians in the city of Rome for Emperor Nero to blame them for the fires which are commemorated in the saying that Nero fiddled while Rome burned.

Within a year or two of the crucifixion, Saul of Tarsus was converted from being a persecutor of the followers of Jesus – the Nazarenes – to his historic role as missionary preacher, thinker, and writer, with his new name of Paul. He founded churches in Asia Minor (modern Turkey) and Greece. He wrote more books than anyone else of what became the New Testament. He ended his life in Rome. He is sometimes called the founder of Christianity. One reason for that description is that his stamp on the thinking and official teaching of the Church remains to this day, while an alternative form of devotion to Jesus, more congenial to Judaism, less given to great titles – Christ, Lord, Son of God – and more to the wisdom attributed to the man from Nazareth, faded away. This process was encouraged by the Roman destruction of the temple in AD 70 and the banishing of Jews from their holy city in AD 135. By the end of the second century there were Christian communities in Syria (including east of the Euphrates), Egypt and, possibly, India; in the Roman province of Africa (Tunisia and Algeria); in Vienne and Lyon on the Rhône; and in parts of Italy as well as Rome. Their language, even in the westernmost areas was Greek, and it was some time before Latin became the vehicle for their liturgy and scholarship. There were periods of persecution, imperially instructed, and those who were willing to be put to death for their faith were venerated as martyrs (literally 'witnesses').

We should dismiss any notion that Christianity spread in a way that could be compared to the modern development of a chain of shops or hotels, each bearing the signs and slogans of the company, with the product marketed according to a carefully prepared plan, and the staff trained and instructed to wear the same uniforms and follow the same techniques in every last outpost of the commercial empire. There is no doubt that Paul and other early missionaries were fired by a desire to spread the news about Jesus throughout 'the whole world', as they knew it. It is also true that, as the years and centuries passed, common factors developed among the congregations: the shared writings forming the New Testament, leadership centred on bishops, and agreement about the understanding of God and Jesus and the core convictions of Christianity. But these things did not happen overnight, and it was not until the fourth and fifth centuries that common statements and interpretations were accepted about the ways in which Christian people spoke about the meaning of God and the implications of Jesus as Christ, Lord, and Saviour. These agreements – or authoritative conclusions, if agreements sound anachronistically democratic – are represented by the Nicene Creed (fourth century) and the doctrine of the Trinity. Four hundred years is quite a long time (if one thinks of the changes between 1600 and now); but the long movement towards authorised vocabulary should not suggest that the heart and worship of the churches in the first three centuries were tentative, half-hearted, or uncertain.

There is an incident described in the Book of Acts which may be helpful in suggesting the way in which doctrine or creeds evolved in these early days. Peter, the leader of the disciples of Jesus, had a dream in which creatures were offered to him to eat, all of them forbidden by Jewish rules on what Jews could eat. He protested that he would refuse to eat anything 'profane or unclean'. A voice then spoke to him and said, 'It is not for you to call profane what God counts clean' (Acts 10: 15). Just then messengers came and asked Peter to visit Cornelius, a Gentile (non-Jew) who wished to hear his message. Peter interpreted his dream as liberating him from his old religious restrictions on mixing with Gentiles; so he went to Cornelius, told him and those with him what he believed about Jesus, and as a result they were baptised and thus entered the Christian community. The news of what had happened reached Christian leaders in Jerusalem, who summoned Peter to explain his conduct. When he did so, the leaders were convinced that Gentiles were indeed eligible to be members of the new community, and 'they gave praise to God', saying, 'This means that God has granted life-giving repentance to the Gentiles also' (Acts 11: 18).

Whether things happened just like that, it is impossible to say. Doubtless more than one incident, and some serious disputation, lay behind the spread of Christianity to Gentiles without requiring them to become Jews first. The order of events, however, is suggestive about how official teaching can develop, and it may be helpful to people concerned in the twenty-first century about whether they can honestly take part in Christian worship. The dream, or vision, or spiritual experience came first. Putting the implication of the experience into practice came next. Only then did the leaders alter an important element in their thinking, to take account of what had occurred.

The point is that worship, or spiritual experience, preceded doctrine. People whose inheritance emphasised the unique oneness of God found themselves speaking of and to Jesus as divine. They did not first develop a rationale for such worship, and then proceed to practise it. The practice came first, and the doctrinal adjustment followed. Worship is possibly more like the experience of beauty or love than like learning a skill, such as flying a plane or operating surgically on the brain. Theories of love and beauty will follow the experience, if at all, and even flying and surgery require practical experience, though some knowledge of the principles beforehand is surely beneficial. To refrain from worship because you have not developed a satisfactory theology is rather like refusing to look at something you have been told is beautiful because you have not developed a philosophy of aesthetics. Such is the line of thought that has led to this attempt to outline the understanding of Christianity.

How could these Christian people make any sense of their practice of hailing Jesus as Lord in a clearly divine lordship, while also recognising the one God of the Hebrew heritage? The author of the fourth Gospel – St John – is often said to have had a 'high Christology', which means that his presentation of Jesus emphasises his divine origin and divine 'connection', much more than the other three Gospels do. The book begins with the section about the divine Word, the agent of creation, which 'became flesh' in Jesus. 'No one has ever seen God; God's only Son, he who is nearest to the Father's heart, has made him known' (John 1: 18). This Gospel contains great claims attributed to Jesus: 'I am the bread of life' (John 6: 48), 'I am the way, the truth and the life' (John 14: 6), 'I and the Father are one' (John 10:

30). He is presented as going to his cross having already said 'I have overcome the world' (John 16: 33). The disciple Thomas, receiving evidence of Christ's risen presence, says 'My Lord and my God' (John 20: 28). It is high Christology to call Jesus God. To say of Jesus that he was Christ the Lord is to say both that he was the special agent of God, and that the agent was God. The long-held belief that it was not permitted to worship anyone or any thing other than God implied that Jesus could not be worshipped unless Jesus was God. But they did worship Jesus; therefore Jesus was God.

The great Saint Augustine (354 – 430) who wrote about the Trinity, God in three persons, Father, Son and Holy Spirit, said that we say there are three persons 'not because that is what we want to say, but so as not to be reduced to silence'. Two comments from twentieth-century theologians may help to amplify not only the inadequacy of such talk but also its usefulness. Ian Ramsey wrote that 'the early Christological and Trinitarian controversies are wrongly seen if they are thought to be concerned with super-scientific discoveries about God, as though the early Fathers had some special high-powered telescope with which to inspect the Godhead. What the early controversies settled were rather rules for our talking, and what came out of them at the end were new symbols for our use, and in particular the Trinitarian formula. The Christian does not have the single word 'God' as his key word. He substitutes for that symbol another; and this other symbol is built out from that focus of our total commitment which is made up of elements of the Christian dispensation.' John Macquarrie, quoting these words of Bishop Ramsey, writes: 'I wish to draw particular attention to the last sentence quoted from Ramsey, for this emphasises, and rightly so, the existential dimension of the Trinitarian language. It is not an objective language, describing a fact laid out for our dispassionate inspection, whether with or without a high-powered telescope. It is a language rooted in existence, in the community's experience of the approach of God. At the same time, it is a language that tries to express an insight into the mystery of God.' [John Macquarrie, *Principles of Christian Theology* (SCM press, 1966), pp174-5.]

Worship leads to doctrine, Jesus is worshipped, and the way the developing church spoke of God had to include Jesus as God. To call Jesus 'God' required them to insist that he had not become divine as Jesus of Nazareth, but that his divinity was in God always. When the power of God to bless them was present before and after the human life of Jesus, they held that that presence was the presence of God himself – and they spoke of that as the Spirit, the Holy Spirit, so much the very presence of God that he could and should be worshipped. Thus, the thinking evolved of three in one and one in three.

It may be that some people find this talk of the Trinity to be unnecessarily complicated, compared to what they see as the happily straightforward use of the word 'God'. Others may find the single word too simple by far, suggesting as it does to them a one-to-one relationship of name to reality, as in the name of a person (Walter Scott, Elvis Presley) or a place (Canberra, Lagos). Whatever else the talk of Father, Son and Holy Spirit does, it does at least challenge that notion of the big man in the sky, which can for some stand in the way of entering the outer doorways of worship, and for others offer attachment to impossible fantasy as an agreeable substitute for a life of faith and trust. The Nicene Creed, named for the Council of Nicaea in 325, and given authoritative confirmation at the Council of Chalcedon in 451, remained through the centuries a basic statement of the belief of the Church. It and the doctrine of the Trinity have been regarded as fundamental expressions of essential Christianity. It is, of course, important to remember that the Creed is said in worship, and that is its principal use, not in study or debate or the teasing out of ideas. It is not 'facts'. Ramsey's telescope may need frequently to be banished.

The spread of Christianity continued in the fourth and fifth centuries. Around 300 the King of Armenia was converted to the Christian faith, and Armenia became the first country to have Christianity as its official religion. The conversion of the Emperor Constantine, who reigned from 306 to 337, led to an increased status for the church, as well as to the development of close identification between the religious and civil authorities. Constantine presided at the church Council of Nicaea in 325, although he had not yet been baptised. He moved his capital from Rome to Byzantium, which he rebuilt and named Constantinople in 330, thus setting the scene for the increasingly distinctive Eastern or Orthodox Church and also for the growing dominance of the Bishop of Rome in the old capital now without its resident emperor. Church growth occurred in Syria, Egypt, Ethiopia, Persia, farther into Asia, as well as in parts of India and Sri Lanka. In Roman Britain Christian worship was observed, and in Ireland Saint Patrick evangelised in the fifth century. In 499 Clovis, King of the Franks, was baptised, and in 598 King Ethelbert of Kent also adopted the faith. The mission to England under Augustine, the first Archbishop of Canterbury, who arrived in 597, and that of Columba, who moved from Ireland to Iona in Scotland in 563, represented the inauguration of the church life of England and Scotland which was to be of such significance in the later development of Christianity in the English-speaking world.

Believing with Bread and Wine

The English writer Evelyn Underhill wrote the following paragraph in a book called *Worship*, published in 1936. It is not exactly how I, writing in 2004, would express the matter. It is, however, one useful way of beginning a consideration of the central element of worship in Christianity, not least because it is written from the standpoint of a committed believer.

Christian worship is never a solitary undertaking. Both on its visible and invisible sides, it has a thoroughly social and organic character. The worshipper, however lonely in appearance, comes before God as a member of a great family: part of the Communion of Saints, living and dead. His own small effort of adoration is offered 'in and for all'. The first words of the Lord's Prayer are always there to remind him of his corporate status and responsibility, in its double aspect. On one hand, he shares the great life and action of the Church, the Divine Society; however he may define that difficult term, or wherever he conceives its frontiers to be drawn. He is immersed in that life, nourished by its traditions, taught, humbled, and upheld by its saints. His personal life of worship, unable for long to maintain itself alone, has behind it two thousand years of spiritual culture, and around it the self-offerings of all devoted souls. Further, his public worship, and commonly his secret devotion too, are steeped in history and tradition; and apart from them, cannot be understood. There are few things more remarkable in Christian history than the continuity through many vicissitudes and under many disguises of the dominant strands in Christian worship. On the other hand, the whole value of this personal life of worship abides in the completeness with which it is purified from all taint of egotism, and the selflessness and simplicity with which it is added to the common store. Here the individual must lose his life to find it; the longing for personal expression, personal experience, safety, joy, must more and more be swallowed up in Charity. For the goal alike of Christian sanctification and Christian worship is the ceaseless self-offering of the Church, in and with Christ her head, to the increase of the glory of God. [Evelyn Underhill, *Worship* (London, Nisbet & Co Ltd., 1936), pp. 81-2]

Although I wish to regard that passage as principally a prelude to saying some things about the Eucharist – the actions involving bread and wine – it also introduces themes about which a few words ought briefly to be written now. First, the idea of believing or worshipping or exercising faith as both shared and individual activities, with a strong emphasis on sharing, is a thread running through the whole experience of Christianity. Despite the emphasis being now more commonly on the individual side of the balance, it remains the background perspective of this book that Christian faith is more a matter of 'what we do' than it is a matter of 'what I think'. Second, the central significance of the church in the Christian religion is matched by the difficulty we have in defining the term Church and in conceiving where its frontiers are to be drawn (to use the writer's language). The church is not the clergy; nor is it equatable to a list of names of those who are, at any time, described as its 'members'. For different purposes, different definitions of 'church' are used. 'Church' can mean an old building, a group of people attached to that building, a collection of such groups (as in 'the Methodist Church'), an individual or group speaking 'on behalf' of 'the Church' (as in 'Church Down on Sloppy Talk'), all Christian people alive at the time of speaking, all Christian people alive and dead. I once heard a preacher quote a priest of the Orthodox tradition: 'Church is when people come together, and Christ and all the saints and angels are there too.' That leads to the third theme in Evelyn Underhill's piece that I should mention: the Communion of Saints. Early on in Christian history much attention was given to significant leaders in the church who had died. There was a special devotion to the places where they died. Rome may have been founding capital city of the Roman Empire; but its importance for Christian people owed much to its being where Peter and Paul met their death. These dead leaders were not only revered for their earthly lives. It was widely believed that after their death they were able to be helpful. If someone was designated your 'patron' saint, that someone was expected to provide good saintly service. The term Communion of Saints suggests a wide company of belief, not easily defined, and not confined to people walking and talking upon earth. In brief, believing is shared as well as individual; the company of believers has many names; and it is a company including, somehow, those who have died – for most of Christian history that was the assumption and perspective of Christian people.

With these emphases Miss Underhill set the scene for our exploration of Christian worship. She also stressed the fact that common threads run through the organised acts of worship of the Christian Church from the beginning until the present day. In no respect is this more true than in the taking and consuming of bread and wine, in the central act which is known by quite a list of titles: Eucharist, Lord's Supper, Holy Communion, Divine Liturgy, Mass. Just think of the huge variety of situations in which that ritual of bread and wine has been carried out. A few examples may serve to indicate both the spread of circumstances and the common ingredients: a first-century congregation in Corinth, Columba visiting some remote promontory on the west coast of Scotland in the sixth century, Charlemagne and his court in Aachen in the ninth century, a papal mass in twelfth-century Rome, an Orthodox cathedral in fourteenth-century Ukraine, Calvin's Geneva in the sixteenth century, Franciscan missions in California in the seventeenth century, African missions in the nineteenth century, Pope John Paul II presiding with a congregation of millions on one of his visits around the globe, and any instance of a few people meeting on a cold winter weekday morning in parish churches and cathedrals in thousands of places at the present time. Everywhere it is at the heart of Christian worship, the event at which people become and are the Church, the mixing of local environment and idiosyncratic understanding with 'the faith once delivered' to the Apostles in Jerusalem in Jesus' time.

What does it mean? Such ceremonies have their background, and one element must certainly be the continuation by the first followers of Jesus of the meals they had with him in Galilee and Jerusalem. His impact must have been extraordinary, and the atmosphere of these gatherings one which they tried to perpetuate. Whatever else the belief in his being raised from death meant, it included the confidence that they continued to eat and drink in his presence even when he was not visibly, physically there as he had been before. We should also recognise that the prevailing culture of the Graeco-Roman first-century world included many instances of people eating and drinking ceremonially with signs and statues representing the various gods in whose presence the people believed themselves to be doing it. Most particularly, however, the development of the ritual meal was influenced by the record of Jesus' Last Supper with his disciples, as written in the first three Gospels, and before them, in the First Epistle to the Corinthians, where we read:

> For the tradition which I handed on to you came to me from
> the Lord himself: that on the night of his arrest the Lord Jesus

took bread, and after giving thanks to God broke it and said:
'This is my body, which is for you; do this in memory of me.'
In the same way, he took the cup after supper, and said: 'This
cup is the new covenant sealed by my blood. Whenever you
drink it, do this in memory of me.' For every time you eat this
bread and drink the cup, you proclaim the death of the Lord,
until he comes. (1 Corinthians 11: 23-26)

That record of Jesus and the disciples in the days before his crucifixion
lies behind all these subsequent acts of worship involving bread and
wine through all these centuries.

That he gave thanks to God follows his Jewish background and
custom, on Sabbath days and festivals, and thanksgiving remains an
essential element in the service. The word Eucharist means 'thanksgiving'. The festival of Passover, however, is especially influential in the
formation of the Christian service. Passover had been the annual act of
commemoration and thanksgiving for the liberation of the Hebrew
people from slavery in Egypt under the leadership of Moses, and Jesus
was presented by early Christian thinkers as the new Moses. As Moses
led the people from Egyptian bondage, Jesus led people to freedom
from fear and sin and death. How he did it, and how he does it, are
matters of endless meditation and speculation. Christian faith holds it
to be true that through him such liberation is offered; that his death was
a critical element in the giving of that freedom; and that the Eucharist
has a central function in bringing the benefit of his gift to people in every
century.

It is also the case that a deeply important aspect of the understanding of these things, one that has been present at all times, must strike
many modern people with puzzlement and even repulsion. It is the
notion of sacrifice, which to many people, for a long time, meant the
killing of an animal in the belief that the very destruction of life made
possible the necessary contact with God, thus restoring the people's
peace and wellbeing after sinful deeds had broken that contact. I dare
say that some Christian people will wish to set a vast distance between
their weekly Eucharist and the splattering of animals' blood in the
Temple in Jerusalem, just as respectable people can pretend that their
notorious criminal uncle is a remotely distant relative (if he exists at
all). Wiser churchgoers may be less squeamish, and, while recognising
that enormous change and refinement have characterised the process
from temple to parish church, our roots remain our roots, and it is
both healthy and humble to refrain from setting the temporary preferences and taste of one era as the sole standard of authenticity and
meaning for every time and place.

As time moved on in Christian history, the theme of sacrifice became increasingly central, and the death of Jesus was seen as the chief sacrifice, remembered or even repeated every time the Eucharist was held. Christ was described as both priest and victim in every Eucharist, and the sacred bread became more closely identified with his body. From the Latin word *hostia* meaning 'victim', the word host came to be used for the bread, and the lifting up of the host in view of the assembled worshippers became the chief part of the service, more important than the people's receiving and consuming of the bread or the wine. By the fourth century, theologians were speaking of the Eucharistic bread as the physical body of Christ, the same body to which Mary gave birth, the body now in heaven. By the eleventh century, thinkers were being charged with heresy if they questioned the claim that every piece of bread in the Eucharist was the genuine physical body of Jesus Christ.

The Church's understanding underwent a deeply significant development in the writing of Thomas Aquinas (Thomas of Aquino, *c.*1225 – 74), who was greatly influenced by the thought of the Greek philosopher Aristotle (384 – 322 BC) whose writings had been preserved by Jewish and Islamic scholars for centuries, during which time they were unknown in Christian Europe. Influenced by Aristotle's distinction between substance and accidents, Thomas developed the theory or doctrine of transubstantiation, according to which the accidents of the bread – its colour, taste, smell, and regular physical features – remain, while its substance becomes Christ's body. Whatever that means, it does not mean that by some miracle the bread becomes Christ's body like a frog turning into a prince in a fairy tale. It is a subtle notion, and as one grapples with the meaning of substance as the underlying essence or the true significance of the bread 'for us', the more one can appreciate that Thomas was not offering a bizarre notion of magical incredulity but, rather, a sensitive attempt to set within philosophical categories what may be a common experience and attitude and conviction of Christian people of any tradition to the central rite of their religion.

What is that experience, which I suggest may be quite common? Sometimes the bread and wine used in Holy Communion are called the elements. It may be that too much attention has been paid to these physical things themselves, and not enough attention to what is done with them. The elements, the ingredients of the ritual or sacrament, might be better understood as the bread <u>and</u> the breaking of it and the sharing of it and the eating of it; the wine <u>and</u> the pouring of it and the sharing of it and the drinking of it. In this perspective, these acts are the vehicles whereby the participants are identified with Christ. It is not so much the bread 'becoming' his body as the act of breaking and eating it together being the means of identification with his life and spirit. The fragments of bread shared speak of the broken life of Christ bringing wholeness to people. The act speaks of love as self-giving, love as the pouring out of oneself, love as that giving which brings wholeness and togetherness to people. Thus, the life of Christ is seen as a key and pattern of good living, in which the model and ideal are not the complete individual, far less the self-made person, but interdependence, sharing with others, mutual acceptance and care. Beyond the words that are used, the service with bread and wine thus communicates in depth that perspective on life which sets self-giving love at the heart of everything. In that sense, we believe that Christianity is natural, suited to our circumstances as human beings.

The Establishment of Christendom

Any attempt to understand the Christian religion in the context of two thousand years must take account of the fact that for much of the history of that religion it possessed the status of establishment. Christianity has been the official religion of the European countries. Not only was it favoured as the chief form of religious expression, it was often required by law that people profess the Christian faith, and other religions – frequently any unauthorised version of Christianity too – were prohibited. The name Christendom is given to the era of Christianity as the one official authorised religion, and also to the part of the world in which that Christian primacy operated. People now look back on Christendom as having ended, and treat it with some embarrassment and even guilt. True Christianity is thought – only by some, to be sure – to be present in the early days of persecution and in our present world, especially when it is a minority movement with few remaining signs of the close identification of church with state, or of the background assumption of a community that Christianity was true, even if some people were vastly more devout and disciplined than others in the fulfilment of its duties and obligations.

As the third century gave way to the fourth, who could have predicted that the company of Christ's followers, subject to occasional bouts of persecution, with intermittent periods of peace and toleration, would soon be set up as the religion of the Empire, with the emperor convening councils of the church, Sunday declared a day of rest, and efforts made to make the boundaries of church districts (or dioceses) more closely coincide with the boundaries of civil administration? It was in 313 that the Emperor Constantine started that process of recognising and establishing Christianity, when he was setting up the new capital, Constantinople, to replace Rome (thereby leaving the Bishop of Rome to be the chief citizen of the old capital – one step towards the development of the primacy of the Bishop, or Pope, within the church in Western Europe). When Constantine called his first council in 325, there were bishops attending who had suffered torture and imprisonment under previous emperors. They had attended previous church gatherings on foot and with great difficulty. Now they came in peace and honour, travelling in the horse-drawn carriages which conveyed the mail around the empire. Constantine himself was not baptised when he convened that council. It was later, and nearer his death, when he confessed Christian faith. The lack of it earlier, however, did not stand in the way of his regarding himself as the chief authority for the Church.

From Constantine until the present day there has not been a time when, in some place, there has not been a close connection between, as people say, 'church and state'. The cathedrals and parish churches of Europe testify to the central significance of the Christian religion in these places. Bishops and other clergy of the church worked closely with kings and queens and regional leaders and were involved in treaties and intrigues, wars and marriages, schemes for building, draining and farming. From early times until fairly recently, in some places the local clergy provided authority and knowledge and often exclusively the ability to read and write. As universities developed, many professors were ordained church ministers, and the respect given to the religious office was indivisible from the recognition that the priest had his uses across a wide range of human activities.

We cannot understand Christianity if we dismiss or bypass Christendom and the establishment of the Christian religion. Is it reasonable to regard so long a phase – some would say it is still with us – as an aberration from the true practice of the faith? Was Christianity perfect before Constantine? Is a minority church inevitably more likely to be truly Christian than a church which has the allegiance of most people in the community? In the balancing of personal conviction and shared corporate believing is Christian faithfulness always to be found where the scales are tipped on the side of the individual and not the communal? It need not be said (it is surely quite obvious) that I am thinking about the establishment of the Christian religion not so much as a historical fact to be analysed but as a present pointer to the nature of the Christianity we are trying to understand.

People in the twenty-first century may hold the opinion that all religious convictions ought to be held by individuals choosing, of their own free will and without undue influence or pressure, to hold them. Such a view may be unrealistic at any time, since the sharing of particular slants or interpretations of Christianity by parents with children is still quite common. It is also a matter of fact, whether modern people like it or not, that the practice of Christianity often spread through kings and other leaders. It happened before Constantine, when Armenia became Christian in the third century. Augustine's mission to England at the end of the sixth century obtained a critical first success through the conversion of King Ethelbert of Kent, the way having been prepared by the king's Christian wife. Within a year Augustine baptised 10,000. How many of these people opted freely for baptism? How could we – or, possibly, even they – know? When Charlemagne (Charles the Great), who was crowned Holy Roman Emperor in Rome on Christmas Day in the year 800, set about conquering the Saxon tribes of what is now Germany, he made Christian allegiance part of the terms of their submission. It is said that he offered a choice: baptism or death. Two centuries later, the long affiliation of the Russian people to the Christian religion came about through the king in his capital of Kiev, after a period in which it seemed possible that he was going to adopt Islam for himself and his people. The custom of rulers determining the character of the religious practice and doctrine of the inhabitants of their territories applied not only to the choice of Christianity but also to the brand or style of it. When the northern European states broke away from allegiance to the pope (as part of what is known as the Reformation) in the sixteenth century, it was neither accidental nor the result of popular voting that some places had Lutheran churches, some Calvinist, and the Church of England took on its new shape. European styles of church have been exported all round the world, and while no imposition regarding the type of church is made on the citizens of the United States of America, it cannot surely be argued that all Southern Baptists are such from uninfluenced free choice, or the children of Polish and Irish immigrants Roman Catholic out of like independent judgement.

In common with the ritual customs of tribes and groups reaching back before recorded history, Christendom shares the fact that in these situations the rituals were the one set of religious practice which the tribe shared. Denominations, sects, and private options do not appear to have been available in ancient Egypt or Assyria; and the assumption would generally be that around Stonehenge and other ancient stone sites the ceremonies which were carried out there were the authorised, accepted pattern of ceremony of the time and place. The parish church in mediaeval Europe was *the* building in the community where the sacred cult was performed. The priest was the parish priest. Tough on deviation it may have been; but religion for the whole community it surely was. There seems to be a thread running through much religious observance, pre-Christian and Christian, in which the strands of holy place, holy ceremony, and holy official for the whole community are constant. We may dislike some of the methods used to create and maintain Christendom while not despising or rejecting the essential notion of the tribal cult, the parish church.

One element of Christendom which should be noticed is the presence of echoes of the position of Israelite religion, as recorded in the Hebrew Bible (the Old Testament). When the leaders of the

Reformation churches set about reorganising their way of doing things, the notion of a holy people following the laws of God found backing in the writings of ancient Israel. John Calvin in Geneva and John Knox in Scotland used the idea of a covenant people in the days of Moses and David to support their view that their places should be places for a committed people living and worshipping as one Christian community, without the liberty of setting up alternative churches to the official church, or permitting non-Christian religions. Once again, it is possible to regret some of the harshness with which attempts were made to implement such ideals while appreciating the long history of the idea that a united community with united expression of religion was somehow natural, certainly ancient.

It is difficult to separate from the establishment of the Christian religion the prominence of the Christian clergy. The development of education in the circumstances of the times led to the clergy occupying positions of great influence, and such positions often led to the corruptions which can accompany unchecked power. On the other hand, enormous benefits were brought through the ordained ministers of the church both to men and women individually, and to the culture and art of the world.

Basic Convictions Settled

The period between the council of church leaders held at Nicaea in 325 and the council held at Chalcedon in 451 saw official acceptance of statements which have served as yardsticks of authentic Christianity throughout the centuries, right up to the present day. One way of appreciating the thinking which lay behind these statements is to look at views or positions which the Church rejected. It is a bit like charting a route for a boat by indicating the rocks and shallows which the boat will need to avoid. Though these rejected views are sometimes called 'heresies', with the implication that everything about them is wrong, there is often some insight and some value in what the 'heretic' is saying, or even just an emphasis which the official position has managed to play down or hide.

In the century and a quarter between the Councils of Nicaea and Chalcedon there were six rocks on which the Church found it helpful to build lighthouses, six stances or interpretations which served the useful purpose of bringing about the reaction which helped define the agreed official position of the Church. Four of the six are identified with four church councils, the other two with the life and thought of Augustine.

1. Arianism

When Constantine called together the bishops who met in Nicaea in 325, his reason was his desire to bring to an end the dissension and squabbling associated with the name of a priest in Alexandria called Arius. The five principal cities of the Church, the cities whose bishops were patriarchs, with authority over wide areas, were Rome, Alexandria, Antioch, Jerusalem, and, after its foundation, Constantinople. Alexandria was noted for its academic community and scholarship. Arius appears to have published little but to have been a clever publicist, with the result that his ideas spread rapidly and attracted a large following. The cause or point which he promoted was the view that Jesus was not fully God. It was not that he went the opposite way and suggested that Jesus was 'just a man'. He claimed that Jesus was divine, and in some sense God, but that he had been created at some point – not that he said that Jesus had a divine element brought into being at his birth, but that the divine element in him had been there long before his human conception and birth, but not for ever. To use the language of the fourth Gospel, St John's, when we read of the Word being made flesh, the Word through which God made everything, Arius accepted that it was that instrument of the world's creation that became a human being in Jesus, but that that Word was created by God and therefore inferior. Jesus would thus require to be understood not as *the* God, the only one fundamental source of life, in human form, but as the lesser divinity in the form of a human life. What the council decided at Nicaea was that Arius was wrong, that Jesus was 'God of God, Light of Light, very God of very God, begotten, not made, being of one substance with the Father; by whom all things were made.'

Does it matter what degree of divinity you attribute to Jesus? If you are concerned not with speculation about the nature of the divine but with the claim that, in the life of Christ, the ultimate heart of life reached towards people to restore to them life at its best, then you will appreciate that it matters that the link is being made credibly by the one claimed to be making it. The authenticity and significance of Jesus Christ matter for Christian people. They will find different forms of language and thought to express that authenticity and significance. But two factors of huge importance lay behind the rejection of Arianism. One is that the Christian belief sees Jesus as ultimate and fundamental, the other is that his significance is not theoretical but practical – not the spread of stimulating ideas so much as the bringing of health and salvation to the souls of people. (In this book I am trying to offer some help in the direction of appreciating what makes Christianity tick. It is important that these fourth and fifth-century debates and disputes be seen as representing what their participants would have regarded as matters of life and death, not of disinterested speculation.)

2. Apollinarianism

The Council of Nicaea in 325 affirmed the divinity of Jesus Christ. The Council of Constantinople in 381 affirmed his humanity. Apollinaris, like so many others through the centuries, tried to answer the question, 'How could Jesus be both human and divine?' The answer he gave was that the divine took over the human mind and soul of Jesus, leaving him only with a divine soul. It is a line of thought which has probably been close to the way devout Christian people have thought of their Lord. They have probably found it hard to think of him having favourite food, a distinctive sense of humour, a capacity of being irritated by situations, or anything that we might regard as unattractive. In 381 they did not attempt to describe Jesus as a balanced, mature, likeable post-Freudian; but they were sure he was genuinely human. They knew that he rested, that he was thirsty, that he could be angry. They also maintained that the claims the church made about Jesus required that he be genuinely human. Some people thought of his human existence as an act of God which altered all the material world, not only all people (a large enough claim in itself, to be sure.) There is a hymn in which, in an English translation from seventh-century Latin, this verse is sung:

> His the nails, the spear, the spitting,
> Reed and vinegar and gall;
> From his patient body pierced
> Blood and water streaming fall:
> Earth and sea and stars and mankind
> By the stream are cleansed all.

Now the scope of Christ's consequences assumed in that verse is gigantic and mysterious. That is the sort of dimension which lay behind the Council of 381 coming down clearly against the teaching of Apollinarius. Gregory of Nazianzus, one of the most influential thinkers in the church at the time, put it thus: 'What has not been assumed cannot be restored.' The thinking behind that remark is that the relationship between God and the human race was impaired or broken, and Jesus repaired and restored it, not only for himself, or for those individuals who followed him, but, somehow, for the whole human race (almost as if a tiny spoonful of cleaning fluid spread throughout a huge lake). The cleaning material had to be capable of mixing with the water in the lake.

3. Nestorianism

Nestorius was a fifth-century bishop of Constantinople – an appointment made by the emperor – whose controversial statements may or may not have been worthy of the title 'heretical'. But then the following generalisation, which may have a grain or two of accuracy in it, might be worth quoting in with him: 'Heretics were often most bitterly persecuted for their least deviation from accepted belief. It was precisely their obstinacy about trifles that irritated the righteous to madness. "Why can they not yield on so trifling a matter?"' [Leo Shestov, *All Things are Possible*, 1905, quoted in *The Oxford Book of Aphorisms* (Oxford University Press, 1983), p. 259.] More relevant to

Nestorius' situation might be the comment that a statement which appears to offend against some matter of wide popular sentiment is likely to provoke resentment and outrage, no matter how marginal the point that is being made. Nestorius first caused trouble by speaking against the growing custom of referring to Mary, the mother of Jesus, as 'Mother of God' or 'God-bearer'. How can God be a three-day-old baby? Even if in Jesus both the divine and the human were fully and truly present, surely it was the human Jesus to whom Mary gave birth? Nestorius was at pains to make clear that he was not denying the divine in Jesus. Looking back from now, we can (or some of us can) feel quite a lot of sympathy with the Bishop of Constantinople. However, devotion to Mary, a feature of Christianity of great prominence throughout the centuries up to the present time, led to his view on the matter receiving much popular hostility.

Nestorius was, of course, pressed for further statements on the right way to speak about the divine and the human in Jesus. One of the commonest features in any dispute is the tendency of both sides to provoke, entice, and even demand of the other further steps along the thought-route for which the first offending claim appeared to be (or was made out by opponents to be) the starting point. He was accused of denying the oneness of Christ, of holding, with the official view, that he was both human and divine, but not that the two were one. He himself denied that he meant that. I suppose we might have had to live on the eastern shores of the Mediterranean in the fifth century to catch every whiff of the controversy.

At the Council of Ephesus in 431 Nestorius was deposed. He died in exile in Egypt. His followers remained faithful to him, and Nestorian churches have remained until the present day, in Syria, Iran and Iraq, as well as in India and America. The identification of Christianity with the Roman Empire, and its continuation centred on Constantinople, needs to be balanced and corrected by the Christianity outwith these imperial boundaries. Churches thrived ever since these early days in Egypt and Ethiopia, and in the regions which for much of the twentieth century lay within the southern parts of the Soviet Union, as well as in the ancient territory around the Rivers Tigris and Euphrates (Mesopotamia), and in the south of India, especially in the state of Kerala. Whatever else the Nestorian crisis stood for, it reminds us of the importance of two elements in Christianity: Jesus' mother as a focus of devotion, and the non-European aspect of the religion. We must not forget that the most significant thinker in the Western Church between the Apostle Paul and the time of Luther and Calvin in the sixteenth century was a man of North Africa, Augustine.

4. Eutychianism

Soon after the Council of Ephesus a controversy arose around
Eutyches, who was accused of claiming that the divine and the human
were completely combined in Christ, with the result that the human
was absorbed by the divine. The significance of the argument lies in its
leading to the adoption of the Creed which is known as the Nicene
Creed, and which remains widely used in worship and as a touchstone
of Christian belief. That adoption of the Creed was agreed by the
council which met at Chalcedon in 451. It has remained in use, with
one addition in the west in the early Middle Ages: the word *filioque*,
meaning 'and from the Son', after 'who proceedeth from the Father'.
The whole Creed, with that added phrase, reads as follows:

> We believe in one God, the Father Almighty, maker of heaven
> and earth, and of all things visible and invisible:
>
> and in one Lord Jesus Christ, the only begotten Son of God,
> begotten of his Father before all worlds, God of God, Light of
> Light, very God of very God, begotten, not made, being of one
> substance with the Father, by whom all things were made:
>
> who, for us men, and for our salvation, came down from
> heaven, and was incarnate by the Holy Ghost of the Virgin
> Mary, and was made man, and was crucified also for us under
> Pontius Pilate. He suffered and was buried; and the third day
> he rose again according to the Scriptures, and ascended into
> heaven, and sitteth on the right hand of the Father. And he
> shall come again with glory to judge both the quick and the
> dead, whose kingdom shall have no end.
>
> And we believe in the Holy Ghost, the Lord and Giver of Life,
> who proceedeth from the Father and the Son; who with the
> Father and the Son together is worshipped and glorified; who
> spake by the prophets.
>
> And we believe one Holy Catholic and Apostolic Church.
>
> We acknowledge one baptism for the remission of sins.
>
> And we look for the resurrection of the dead, and the life of
> the world to come.

We must consider some parts of the Creed in due course, including the
word *filioque*, not least because of the growing division which separated
the eastern part of the Church centred on Constantinople from the
western part whose centre was Rome. Deeply important in the intellectual confidence of the Western Church was the contribution made by
Augustine, Bishop of Hippo in North Africa.

5. Donatism

When Augustine became bishop in Hippo in 396, he found himself immediately involved in a major controversy which had brought severe disturbance and division to the church in North Africa. Several Roman emperors had imposed heavy penalties on Christians, and bishops and other leaders were tortured and killed when they refused to deny their faith. In the last such time of persecution, under the Emperor Diocletian at the beginning of the fourth century, the clergy were ordered to give up their bibles to be burned. Some refused to do so, and suffered severely. Donatus was a bishop of Carthage who gave it as his view that not only had the bishops who handed over their bibles been unfaithful, but also those who were ordained and consecrated by them carried the stain of infidelity and were therefore not proper bishops and priests. A separate Donatist church was led by those whose professional ancestry included none of the 'unfaithful' ones, and in some places it was the major church of the area. The principal issue became that of priestly purity: did the validity of a sacrament – such as the Eucharist or Holy Communion – depend on the moral quality of the person who presided? Could a wicked priest celebrate a valid sacrament? Under Augustine's leadership the matter was resolved, on the side of the judgement that the presiding minister was merely the instrument of God's action, and that the personal virtue of the individual minister was not essential to the sacrament being a true sacrament. Augustine was concerned to promote and defend the unity of the Catholic Church, as the word 'Catholic' was coming to be used, for the whole organised church roughly following the territory of the Empire, whose centre had moved from Rome to Constantinople. Five centuries later, the word would refer to the western part, Constantinople becoming the home city of the eastern, 'Orthodox' part of the old empire lands. The defeat of Donatism expressed that concern for unity as well as the important perspective on sacraments and the clergy. Though dependence on God and not on 'good' priests was a valuable point, it had the drawback of encouraging, in later times, a rather mechanical or even magical approach to worship, and an uncritical respect for clerical hierarchy. What mattered to Augustine, possibly more than any other thing, was the dependence of the believer on God, whose grace he saw as making human goodness possible.

6. Pelagianism

Pelagius (c. 360 – 420) was British (or possibly Irish), and is thought to have been a monk (though doubts have been expressed about whether the monastic attribution was genuine). He taught in

Rome and then fled with others to North Africa after the Visigoth invasion and plundering of Rome in 410. He attracted followers, but his teaching was declared heretical by the Council of Ephesus in 431. Although Augustine led the assault on what Pelagius taught, the Augustinian position was well developed before Pelagius came on the scene. The controversy, however, polarised the issue which divided them. It was an issue of great significance for Christian thought and attitudes, and for teaching and judgement on matters of behaviour, especially sexual matters, across the centuries until the present day.

The critical question concerned the extent to which people were free and able to please God and live good lives. It was widely believed that the human race was sinful, ever since Adam, the first man, sinned. The sinful nature of people was transmitted from generation to generation, from parents to children. (Whether that view requires a belief that the creation story at the beginning of the Bible is to be treated as history, or rather as a dramatic way of talking about essential humanity, is another matter.) Augustine regarded his conversion to Christian faith as a rescue, through God's deliberate action, not only from a lack of faith but from a self-indulgent past of youthful sexual licence. He strongly held that it was by God's grace that people kept faith with him, and that the living of a good life, made possible by divine grace, included sexual discipline as a central element. These notes have sounded loudly through the church of the west – that is, Catholic as distinct from (eastern) Orthodox, and, after the sixteenth century, Catholic (or Roman Catholic) and Protestant.

The teaching of Pelagius must seem to many modern people to be sensible and hard to oppose. He accepted that people were sinful, since Adam, but that we have enough freedom to go quite a long way along the road of pleasing God and living good lives. He could not accept Augustine's view that all people are a 'mass of corruption', and all, without exception, deserved eternal damnation. A liberal conjunction of the two positions, along the lines of saying that our lives are gifts and not achievements, and that our ability to do good is the result of gifts, so that we can see the help of God in and through everything that is good about us, would have cut no ice with Augustine. Perhaps one fundamental emphasis which might help us sympathise with the 'winning side' is the conviction that God is not a detached, remote, external power – the giant beyond the sky – but is within us and around us; that dependence on him is not so much like that of a weak old slave on a powerful, kindly, slave-owner as like the dependence of plants on sun and water, something thoroughly natural.

I have put together these six issues which helped define and direct the Church's teaching and character for centuries to come. The middle of the fifth century saw much of the intellectual development still in the east, in Constantinople assisted by Alexandria and Antioch, but with strong signs of the growing place of the church based on Rome and on the Latin language. We should remember that the development of Latin as the language of theology is headed by two men of North Africa, Tertullian (of Carthage, second century) and Augustine.

Living a Devoted Life

The Christianity which developed during its first five centuries did not have debate and decision about the best ways of speaking about God, Christ, and the Holy Spirit as its sole or chief feature. The search for agreement on these matters was important because it served Christian devotion – how to worship and how to live as followers of Jesus Christ. We know the 'big names'; but we must keep in mind the thousands of believers who went to church week by week, and who tried to follow a way of life appropriate to Christian people.

The record of Jesus' teaching transmitted through the pens and the minds of Matthew, Mark, Luke and John is more open and suggestive than precise and prescriptive. It caused some comment when Margaret Thatcher, British Prime Minister in the 1980s, who had as a student conducted services in Methodist churches, said that the Parable of the Good Samaritan in St Luke's Gospel implied a form of capitalism, since the Samaritan would not have been able to pay the innkeeper to care for the wounded traveller if he had not made enough money to allow him to do so. Loving your neighbour sounds fine. The capacity of the human mind to define the words to fit one's own convenience is considerable. There are few things about which Jesus appears to have given clear rules or advice concerning conduct. That situation is, for many people, a happy one, because it treats Christian people as free men and women, with the liberty and duty to work out in changing circumstances what the right thing is for them to do. A rule book which left no room for thought and judgement would leave the believer as a robot, a slave, an unthinking machine.

It is true that in his letters in the New Testament Saint Paul gives advice on moral matters to the young congregations to whom he wrote, advocating self-discipline and generosity, but it is also true that in the earliest days the church lived in an atmosphere of expecting some great concluding glory on earth, represented by the return of Jesus and the inauguration of his rule or empire throughout the world. It was even suggested that it would be good not to procreate children, since things were all going to end soon. But the business of getting on with life in the continuing world of human affairs soon put the sense of living in an interim period well into the background, though Christians continued to read and hear their Scriptures, as they still do. People are good at letting some fine words pass them by, or altering their meaning to something they feel they are able to digest.

Yet devotion to Jesus was central to the development of standards and practices among Christian people. There was a considerable blurring of distinctions of class and wealth. Money was systematically collected to give to poor people, and no preference was shown to members of the church over others who were poverty-stricken. There was general opposition to capital punishment, and certain jobs were regarded as incompatible with allegiance to Christ.

The equality of women with men was held somewhat ambiguously, in that all Christian people, male and female, were believed to be 'one in Christ', equally loved by God, equally the recipients of divine grace and help, but with different roles in church and daily living. The significance of women in the Gospels and the early church remains considerable. Women were among the followers of Jesus in Galilee, and some came with him to Jerusalem and were there at the time of his crucifixion. The woman who anointed Jesus' feet is defended by him for her lavish display, and the woman who contributes her last mite is commended, generosity being properly measured not by the amounts people give, but by the amounts they retain. The figure of Mary Magdalene has provoked artistic piety through the centuries, second only to the dominating presence and image of Jesus' mother, Mary. It was to women, on the first Easter morning, that the news of the resurrection was first given, according to the Gospels. Though women were not given the position of official leadership or appointed bishops or priests, the grounds for not standing in the way of such appointments were there in the New Testament (as the supporters of women's ordination in the twentieth century would surely affirm).

Men were expected to be faithful to their wives – which was quite a change, in a world where fidelity was often expected of wives only.

How did it come about that these groups of men and women, devoted to Christ, turned into an international organisation dominated by professional clergy, a large chunk of the show being dominated by one super-official within the professional clergy? The question may seem a fair one, even if its language is less than reverential, but it smacks of more than a hint of romantic reconstruction of the church's earliest days. The Apostle Paul did not found twentieth-century communes in which every member had a vote and majority decisions were binding. From the start, the Apostles retained a watching interest in the churches which they had founded, and it was not surprising that others became accepted to fill the gap left by the founding fathers. Did they need a priestly group who were alone allowed to administer the sacraments? The question may seem pointless, though it might be worth suggesting that it will not seem pointless to those who do not wish to accept that Christianity is a religion. What is certainly the case is that bishops became common among the presbyters who had been chosen in the towns where there were churches (churches being an urban development). Bishops shared in the consecration of new bishops, and uniformity became inevitable to avoid discrepancies in the way people were treated from place to place – including the imposition of penalties for grave offences. The question of whether Christianity could have been less clergy-ridden is not easily answered, except by those who think the charge is largely unfounded.

The clergy were expected to be good men who could be regarded as examples by the members. Saints and martyrs were certainly regarded with great veneration from an early period. Martyrs were people who were put to death for their Christian allegiance. The word martyr means witness, and they were seen to bear witness to their commitment to Christ, as well as bearing witness to his death by dying. In the seventh chapter of Acts the death of Stephen is described. Like Jesus, he forgives his murderers. Stephen is regarded as the first martyr. The future Apostle Paul was present, and although it is not stated specifically that the experience of Stephen's death and his manner of dying led to Paul's conversion to the Christianity which he had vigorously opposed, nothing is written which would deny such a connection. It certainly accords with the conviction that faithfulness to the extent of martyrdom was instrumental in bringing others to Christian allegiance. 'The blood of the martyrs is the seed of the church' is a famous claim made by Tertullian, who lived in Carthage in North Africa in the second and third centuries and was a leading theologian, the first to write in Latin (and second only to Augustine, a fellow North African, as major thinker of the western, Latin-speaking, increasingly Rome-centred, part of the church).

During the three centuries before Constantine, persecution of Christians happened from time to time. It was not uncommon for the execution of penalties, especially death, to be carried out with reluctance and puzzlement by Roman officials who could not understand why Christians were unwilling to obey the emperor and honour him and other gods as symbolic gestures intended to maintain the unity of the empire. A small act to save one's life, they saw it. In the middle of the second century, Polycarp, Bishop of Smyrna, was offered escape from death when the Roman governor told him he would be set free if he took the imperial oath. The bishop replied that he would rather die than deny the Lord to whom he had been faithful for eighty-two years. Polycarp's death and the account of his manner as he approached it were deeply influential. Some believers even sought death by martyrdom, wishing one another the speedy acquisition of the crown which they expected, as martyrs, to receive after death. The search for martyrdom was not admired by all church leaders, however, and the official view became one of admiring the bravery and faith of those who refused to make compromises under threat of persecution, while not supporting any revelling in suffering for its own sake, or virtually sending invitations to the authorities saying 'Come and persecute me'. It remains possible, in tolerant liberal circles today, for devout Christian believers to regard themselves as enduring the hostility of others on account of their faith, when the others are reacting adversely not to the Christian content of their faith but to elements of insensitivity and lack of respect for opponents, which can always be a risk of deep religious commitment, especially when it lacks humour. That should not prevent us from recognising that in today's world, in recent decades, people have paid severe penalties on account of Christian commitment, especially in the face of oppressive governments, and the word martyr has been used of them.

The veneration of martyrs led to the recognition of a wider category among Christian people who had died, and to invoking their help – not only in the sense that the living could find guidance and wisdom from recalling the virtues and faithfulness of those who had died, but in the sense of believing that the dead, in the next world, were able to give help to the living, by interceding on their behalf with God or by assisting directly, and that such help could come in response to the requests made by the living. When we speak of devotion to the saints, we are speaking of that strong sense of their active contemporary assistance.

The custom of honouring saints on a regular, annual basis, on a particular day, goes back far. Supporters of the martyred Polycarp vowed to hold the anniversary of his death as a birthday celebration of his new life as a martyr. As to the selection of people to be called saints, the development was popular and unsystematic for centuries. Bishops often played a part, but the elevation of popular heroes and heroines operated, then as now, with a momentum of its own. Eventually, the selection of saints became something that was vetted and authorised by Rome, but it was not until the thirteenth century that that central control, still in force in the Roman Catholic Church, became fully established. Some saints were widely accepted as saints from early on, while others were revered only within the small area where they were remembered. For millions of Christian people the rituals and emphases of the veneration of saints have been a deeply important part of their religion – and, most importantly, their veneration of Mary, the Lord's mother.

In the Reformation of the sixteenth century, the parts of the church which have been generally called Protestant were, on the whole, opposed to the role the saints had played in worship and piety, and many whose background is 'Protestant' may find that side of religion puzzling, unacceptable, or even offensive. Others, seeking to understand the Christian religion better, will also have their reactions and questions. What can, I suggest, seem inconsistent is the coupling of an apparent ease in speaking of God, in terms which suggest a human-like person, with a total rejection of the other inhabitants of our ancestors' 'other world' – in brief, angels, saints, and devils. There is some consistency in declining all talk of the other world, heaven and hell, including reference to God. But singling God out as if we were talking of some observable phenomenon, while rejecting other references possessing the semblance of 'people-talk' on the ground that they are not 'real', may leave us without important elements of experience on the grounds that we do not like their names, while trapping the lonely God on the wrong side of an important distinction. But this is probably no problem to the Muslim women who kneel at a shrine to the Virgin Mary in Baghdad asking her to help them conceive a child.

Devotion to Christ has usually been part of people's lives, and even when that devotion affected and gave focus to the other aspects of their lives, these other aspects have continued. Christian people have learned a skill, earned a living, fallen in love, married and had children, shared in the common responsibilities of a village or town, and kept company in shops and sport and work with people whose religious commitment was quite different from theirs. A movement began in the fourth century, however, which encouraged people to cut themselves off from ordinary life, and live as monks or nuns. The movement began in Egypt – once again we should remember that much of the detail of Christian thought and practice developed in North Africa and western Asia – and is thought to have started with Anthony, who moved farther and farther away from towns and people in order to be alone, a hermit for God. Renunciation of pleasure, and especially of sex, had already been advocated by some in the church. Anthony carried it farther, and separated himself from people. Others followed him, and devised means of being cut off from regular society. One, Simon, took to living on top of a high pillar, and had food drawn up by a rope. Individual hermits lived in huts or caves in the Egyptian desert. It was in Egypt, also, that the first monastery was formed, when Pachomius gathered men together in a dedicated community around 320. The movement was supported by Basil, the leading thinker, who wrote a Rule of Discipline in the fourth century which remains authoritative for monasteries of the Greek Orthodox tradition today.

Monasteries were founded in what are now Greece, Italy and France, as well as in Asia Minor and North Africa. The scholar Jerome, in a monastery in Bethlehem, translated the Bible from Hebrew and Greek into Latin: this was the version of the Bible used in Catholic churches for more than fifteen hundred years, until the second half of the twentieth century. In 529 at Monte Cassino, south of Rome, Benedict founded a monastery and wrote for it the Rule, or set of duties and details of monastic life, which has governed the many Benedictine monasteries that followed Monte Cassino. Other traditions evolved, but the Benedictine Rule has affected monastic life as nothing else. He set out times of worship, ways of solving disputes, insistence on poverty, chastity, and obedience, and required that monasteries be as self-sufficient as possible, growing their own food and making their own wine. Monasteries also became places of study, where manuscripts were copied and studied, and the writings of the Church Fathers, as well as of classical Rome, were preserved. During what are sometimes called the Dark Ages, the monasteries kept scholarship alive and developed agricultural and other skills. Their contribution to civilised life has been enormous.

Many Christian people would find monastic life unappealing, and would see their Christian duty as being in the middle of ordinary life. Patterns of human living have changed, however, and the nuclear family is by no means the norm in the western world. This is possibly a time to ask questions about the extent of the variety that is possible in the sharing of life. It may also be a time for asking about the importance of contemplation, and offering places for others to retreat and be refreshed for living.

Jesus the Saviour

Throughout the English-speaking world this hymn is sung on Good Friday, the day on which the crucifixion is commemorated, and at other times too. It was written for children, but that should not prevent some contemplation of its language bringing benefit to people of any age.

> There is a green hill far away
> Without a city wall,
> Where the dear Lord was crucified,
> Who died to save us all.
>
> We may not know, we cannot tell
> What pains he had to bear;
> But we believe it was for us
> He hung and suffered there.
>
> He died that we might be forgiven,
> He died to make us good,
> That we might go at last to heaven,
> Saved by his precious blood.
>
> There was no other good enough
> To pay the price of sin;
> He only could unlock the gate
> Of heaven, and let us in.
>
> O dearly, dearly has he loved,
> And we must love him too;
> And trust in his redeeming blood,
> And try his works to do.

Mrs Cecil F. Alexander, *c.*1838 (1818 – 1895).
First published in *Hymns for Little Children,* 1848.

Although the Church wrestled with questions about the divine and the human in Jesus, and about the nature of the Trinity, no similar process occurred in relation to what is often called the 'saving work of

Christ'. Yet there is not the slightest doubt that the writers of the New Testament believed that benefit and blessing of incomparable magnitude had come to believers through his death and resurrection. Preachers and writers continued to proclaim that conviction, but no attempt was made to reach a single authorised statement of what the Church believed about it. As church buildings became increasingly important, and as they were seen to have special power through relics of saints – small fragments of the saint's body, or of objects connected with the saint – the Eucharist or Mass remained the most potent of all, and the consecrated bread, the host, the most venerated object in the church. Why? It was because the sacrifice of Christ on the cross on Good Friday was present to bless the worshippers. But what was the sacrifice of Christ, and how did it bless the people?

Perhaps 'for us' is about as near as we can get to putting into words the consequences of Christ's death. They certainly repeat the lines in the Nicene creed, that he became man 'for us' and that he was crucified 'for us'. This little phrase indicates, certainly, that Christ's suffering had a purpose, that it was not suffering for its own sake, but also, possibly, that his suffering was vicarious, namely undergone by him in our stead. That is a notion that has been around in relation to Christ and Christians for a long time. It is not straightforward. I can perfectly well imagine doing something unpleasant which needs to be done, in order that a friend is relieved of the need to do it. But how can the death of Christ relieve me and the others now? By being crucified, did he stop me being crucified? It seems a strange notion.

The fifty-third chapter of the book called Isaiah in the Bible tells of a 'servant' who suffers 'for' others. 'He was wounded for our transgressions, he was bruised for our iniquities, the chastisement of our peace was upon him, and with his stripes we are healed' (Isaiah 53: 5). Christian thinkers have used that chapter to interpret the death of Christ ever since the New Testament was being written. The chapter continues: 'All we like sheep have gone astray; we have turned every one to his own way; and the Lord has laid on him the iniquity of us all.' Strange, mysterious ideas – apart from their meaning, they remind us of the tendency of people to use the imagery and language that they have available, to describe, or even to perceive, a new and puzzling experience. It probably follows that if we lack a good stock of ways of saying things, we will find the future harder to describe, or even, in part, to experience.

We sing that he 'died to save us all'. There are, in the New Testament, ways of speaking about the significance of Christ which cover both saving people *for* and saving them *from*. The Parable of the Prodigal Son presents God as a welcoming, forgiving father who loves his children, irrespective of how good or faithful they have been. Jesus can be seen as the messenger of that assurance and welcome. The salvation which he offers is an offer of a new and restored relationship with God. The claim is made that, in Christ, God was reconciling the world to himself, not just the believers. How could a man's execution repair a broken link between heaven and earth? One answer to the question is in the last verse of the hymn:

> O dearly, dearly, has he loved,
> And we must love him too.

It has been suggested that the extent of God's love for people was shown by Jesus' willingness to die. Perhaps it is a thought better sung in a hymn than analysed too carefully. Certainly, it can be argued that his being executed by Jewish and Roman officials working together is not incompatible with his death also being the expression of divine love, since the two explanations are of differing types, and therefore not alternatives.

It was suggested by several writers in the first two centuries that Jesus not only saved people *for* a good relationship with God, and all that that may be held to bring, but *from* the clutches of the Devil. Sometimes this was described as a fight in which 'the young Prince of Glory' took on the Prince of Darkness, who was holding the human race captive, and won, thereby ensuring their release.

The death of Christ was also seen in early church writing as a form of payment which was made to the Devil to release people. Slaves were sometimes bought from slavery to liberty, and the idea of freed slaves lies behind the idea of Christ as Redeemer, the one who 'pays the price'. How did the human race become enslaved? By the fall of Adam, the first man, many would have replied, adding that all of Adam's successors have also sinned, thereby adding to their enslavement to evil, and to the Evil One.

But the concept of paying the price of sin does not require that the payment is made to the Devil. One of the most influential contributions to Christian thinking on this matter was made by Anselm, who was Archbishop of Canterbury in the eleventh century. His interpretation of the saving work of Christ was that God required the human race to serve him, but that the service which was needed could be given only by someone who was both divine and human. The point requires a little filling out.

Anselm was born in Lombardy, in the north of Italy, in about 1033. He moved to France and became a monk at the Abbey of Bec in Normandy, where the abbot was a fellow Lombard, Lanfranc, who later became Archbishop of Canterbury. Anselm developed a considerable reputation as a thinker and writer, and some have called him the ablest theologian between Augustine in the fifth century and Thomas Aquinas in the thirteenth. Unlike many of his predecessors as theologians, he tended to depend not so much on biblical quotations to present his arguments as on the rational coherence of the arguments themselves. He became Abbot of Bec after the death of Lanfranc's successor and then, on Lanfranc's death, succeeded him at Canterbury. His time as archbishop was marked by courageous stands against the two kings who followed William the Conqueror, and he twice went into exile in France and Italy. It should not go unnoticed that the state of Christian Europe was such that archbishops on occasion fled for their lives, or that it was quite unremarkable for two successive Archbishops of Canterbury to be Italian. The language of the church was, of course, Latin, whatever other local languages churchmen spoke. It should also be borne in mind that Anselm was, throughout his time as archbishop, deeply committed to the establishment and perpetuation of the see of Canterbury as the centre of a church province which would include not only the whole of England, but Wales, Scotland and Ireland too. It is arguable that if he had succeeded, the central authority of the popes might have been balanced by strong provincial leaders. It is certainly claimed that the loss of the North African church, centred on Carthage, after the rise of Islam, removed that section of the church in the west most able to stand up to the authority of Rome and challenge its bishops. Anselm's failure to establish his province of the British Isles can therefore stand with the decline of Christian Carthage as markers of the rise of the papacy. The impact of the British Isles project on the political and other arrangements of the area can only be the subject of imaginative speculation.

It was this Anselm who wrote *Cur Deus Homo* (Why God became Man). The honour which the human race should give to God needs to be given by the human race. Yet the circumstances of what it means to be human result in no human person being able to give that service or honour. Therefore, the human who gives it must also be divine; and the only way that can happen is for someone to be both human and divine. Thus, in extreme abbreviation, Anselm distances himself from all talk about the death of Christ being a bribe to the Devil. He also separates himself from those who regard the death of Christ as a penalty or punishment paid on behalf of the human race. While he would accept Mrs Alexander's assertion that 'There was no other good enough', he would have difficulty with 'To pay the price of sin', if that line is understood to refer to the serving of a penal sentence.

What about the picture of Jesus unlocking the gate of heaven, and letting us in? The word atonement is often used to speak of the benefit to the believer of Christ's death. It means the bringing together of people with God (at-one-ment). If a person focuses worship on or through the man Jesus, then that person is seeing God in Jesus, and thus the human person is brought close to God. If, in the Eucharist, the taking and sharing of bread and wine bring identification of the individual worshipper with Jesus Christ and with God through Christ, then the death of Christ, set forth in the sacrament, becomes the channel of worship and identification.

But what about the last two lines of the hymn? With 'his redeeming blood' we are back in the world of animal sacrifice, a world recalled in every Eucharist in which the Agnus Dei is said or sung: 'Lamb of God, that takest away the sins of the world, have mercy upon us; grant us thy peace.' That prayer to Christ is derived from the Gospel of St John, where John the Baptist says of Jesus, 'Behold the Lamb of God, who takes away the sin of the world' (John 1: 29). It has been suggested (to my mind, wholly persuasively) that the reason for the church not working out an agreed statement on the Atonement (as was done for the Incarnation) is that the Eucharist is the means, far better than any verbal statement, by which the thrust and value of Christ's life and purpose are taken on board by the worshippers, who somehow make them their own. There, at the Holy Table, are things and people – bread and wine, and the mixture of character and experience, age and insight, of any human group. Better it is that the meaning of Christ's life be given in practice than accounted in books, however valuable the latter may be in their place and at their level.

Possibly too frequently in Christian history, the death of Jesus Christ has been separated from his life before he died. Like the lamb to which he was compared, he may be thought to be pure and without blemish, but these qualities seem more ex officio than actual descriptions of the man. It is true that the four Gospels concentrate on the last week of this life, and the epistles make few references to what went before that week. But enough sketching is given of a real person with real priorities and attitudes to behaviour and religion for us to colour in the Eucharistic presentation of Christ with specific yardsticks of behaviour and attitude, enough to provoke and challenge us, and help us carry out the last line of the hymn, 'and try his works to do'.

What cannot be denied is that Christian devotion has at times appeared to adopt an almost amoral attitude to the sacraments and to the cross, as if there were no implications for behaviour in being associated with them, and as if the cross as an object, or a sign made with a hand in the air, possessed a power quite distinct from God and

Christ. Doubtless such an appearance would be widely denied. What is certain is the enormous confidence, from early times, which many Christian people have had in the sign of the cross and in crosses, physical reproductions, usually in miniature, of the gibbet on which Jesus was killed. There is a well-known legend of Helena, the mother of Constantine, going to Jerusalem in the third century, finding the cross on which Jesus died, and sending part of it to her son. It is said that he was so sure that wherever the true cross was would be safe that he had the wood placed within his statue at the heart of Constantinople, and that he had the nails which had held Christ's hands made into bridle-bits and a helmet which he wore to battle. After that, pieces of wood, regarded as portions of the true cross, were distributed and sold all over the place, as the devotion to relics grew into a significant feature of church life through the Middle Ages.

You do not have to go along with Helena, however, to approve the use of the cross symbol on spires and hymn books, national flags and gravestones, or suspended on chains round the necks of bishops and teenage girls. And if we read, with raised eyebrows, of ancient saints by the sign of the cross turning beasts into sleepy tabby cats, there is no requirement that we treat the tales as facts: but there is, perhaps, an invitation to recognise that words and reasoned thought do not contain all ways of making meaning known and calling to our aid the things which are for us the truest and the best.

West and East

From the cross we may turn to the Crusades. A crusader was someone who wore a cross (*crux*) as a sign that he had 'taken up the cross' in devotion to Christ to take Jerusalem and the sacred places of the Bible back from the hands of Muslims who had captured the city in 637. The Crusades were military expeditions undertaken in the eleventh, twelfth and thirteenth centuries. Writing, even briefly, about them provides an opportunity of linking some of the chief elements in Christianity in the thousand years between the Council of Chalcedon and the Reformation: the rise of Islam, the schism between the Greek-language church of the eastern Mediterranean and the Latin church whose chief place was Rome, the position of the papacy and the growing differences between east and west, the place of pilgrimages, and the powers of state and church in a developing Europe.

Like Helena, many believers travelled to Palestine in order to be where Jesus lived, and the idea grew at an early stage that such a journey was more than a quest for information. It was seen as an act of piety, both an expression of faith and a way of strengthening faith. In 614 Persian armies captured Jerusalem, but the Emperor took the city back into 'Christian' hands in 628. In 637, however, Arab forces took the city and Muslims occupied it, allowing both Christians and Jews to practise their religion, the Jews being permitted entry into the city for the first time in almost five hundred years. (Over the following fourteen centuries there would occur many instances of broad tolerance by Muslim authorities to Christians and Jews.) The pilgrimages continued, but when Turkish forces took Jerusalem from the Arabs, both Muslims, in 1071 life became more difficult for Christians there, and the idea of help coming from the West was put forward. In 1095 Pope Urban II called for the conquest of Jerusalem. This summons came at a time when relations between Christianity (Rome) and Christianity (Constantinople) were not good.

The move of the imperial court to Constantinople early in the fourth century led to the development of a distinctive style and substance in the worship and administration of the church there and in the eastern part of the empire, while the church in Rome and those places connected to Rome continued in the way it was going, succeeding imperial Rome as the centre of a church empire of the West. The ecclesiastical world whose centre was Constantinople was, however, a loose federation of churches rather than a tightly controlled unity, and something of that has remained true of Orthodox churches until the present day. When we speak of the Christian Church before the sixteenth century, we speak of the Catholic Church until the eleventh century, after which we think of the word Catholic applying to the West, increasingly under the authority of Rome, while the Greek-speaking churches of the East are known as Orthodox. Since the sixteenth century, the division of all churches is into Catholic (or Roman Catholic), Orthodox, and all the others, who are often described together as Protestant (though the word appeals more to some than to others).

Monasticism started in Egypt and Syria and monasteries, for men, and also similar houses for women, have been an important part of Orthodoxy. Characteristic of monastic life, as well as of the life of town and village churches, has been a high regard for rich and mystical worship, with frequent references to the Trinity where others might say God, as in 'the world was created by the Holy Trinity', and a fond and reverent familiarity with talk of the Holy Spirit. It was that devotion to the Holy Spirit which lay at the heart of one of the principal points of disagreement which led to the breach between East and West, usually dated to the year 1054, when the pope's representative issued an anathema against the Patriarch of Constantinople, who responded by anathematising the papal representative – that is, each cursed and banished the other. But the process inevitably lasted for far more than a year. The practice had started, it seems in Spain, in the sixth century, of adding one word to the Creed, where it says that the Church believes in the Holy Spirit 'who proceeds from the Father'. The added word is *filioque*, which means 'and from the Son'. The people who added *filioque* were therefore saying that the Spirit comes from Father and Son. It seems that in the East that addition was taken to be a slight on the Holy Spirit, putting the Holy Spirit in a category less significant than that of the Son, that is, Christ. It is a matter about which great heat can be produced, even now.

By the time of the mutual cursing, the styles of the two areas were already markedly different. The style of the East was one of diversity and conciliar decision-making, while, in the West, unification and central authority in one person were much more the way things were going. One important difference is that while under Rome priests were and are forbidden to marry, in Orthodox churches only the bishops are required to be celibate, and are therefore chosen from among the monks, while the overwhelming majority of parish clergy are married men with families. Another important and obvious difference is the place of icons in Orthodox churches. Icons are pictures of Jesus Christ, or of angels, or of saints, including, especially, Mary, the mother of Jesus. Although there were two periods in the ninth century when icons were banned (their opponents being the iconoclasts, a word in use by many who might not be able to say much about its origin), icons have been deeply valued in the piety of church and home. The worshipper believes that the person in the picture is brought near, that things of creation are rightly used to express the divine, and that communication of the deep mysteries of the faith should not be confined to words and rational thought. It is also claimed that icons testify to a great distinction between Orthodoxy and both the Catholic and Protestant churches: namely, since Augustine, the latter have regarded the world, its creation and matter, as fundamentally flawed, while to the Orthodox mind nature is essentially good. A similar point is sometimes made – that the Orthodox East focuses on Incarnation, Transfiguration, Ascension, while the Catholic West has its mind on Redemption and the Cross. Doubtless, these points can be called over-simplified. On the other hand, a matter can be presented in so balanced a way, hedged about with qualifications, that the essential point of the claim may be missed. One of the consequences of the East – West difference about whether earthly things are good or bad may be a heavy emphasis on sin and guilt in the West. Another may be the greater readiness of the church in the West, at times, to criticise and oppose the state, believing that all human activity is flawed, whereas the churches of the Orthodox tradition may have a greater inclination to support and defend the state, in continuity with the Constantinian doctrine that the emperor on earth had, at human level, the same sort of responsibility for all human matters as God in heaven had over all matters in heaven and on earth. Such a view could well lead to a somewhat rose-tinted attitude to governments and political power. From the end of the Second World War (1939 – 45) the Soviet Union's sway in Eastern Europe (the countries of the Warsaw pact, or the Iron Curtain countries) lasted until the collapse of the Berlin Wall in 1989 and the restoration to independence of these nations. Relations between communist leaders and churches varied from country to country and from time to time. The attitude of Orthodox leaders and Catholic leaders seems, at a distance and on the surface, to reflect the difference of emphasis which I have just sketched. Those of us, however, who have never faced life-threatening hostility to our religious affiliation or our freedom of speech would be wise to hesitate before judging the conduct of others who have been placed in such situations.

The Crusades had little short-term success, and none that lasted. They left a romantic memory of gallant knights on a noble mission, though there was nothing unreal about the success of the armies of Islam taking over territory which had been within the Roman Empire. By 750 they controlled Arabia, Egypt, Syria, Iraq, North Africa, Turkey and Persia. Soon after that there were Muslim colonies in Italy. Many of the lands in which the Eastern (Orthodox) Church had flourished were now in Muslim hands, including three of the five cities of patriarchs (church leaders with responsibility over their areas, and carrying great prestige): Alexandria, Antioch and Jerusalem. It would be fair to say that Constantinople was beginning to feel a little isolated and rather threatened, though it was not until 1453 that Turkish armies captured the city. Its weak position in the preceding centuries was made worse by an act which soured the already bitter feelings towards Rome. In 1204 the Fourth Crusade ended with the siege, capture, and looting of the city. It appears that the Venetians, who provided the ships for the crusaders, diverted them to Constantinople and persuaded them to become involved in a local dispute there, ending in thoroughly disreputable behaviour and the capture of the city until 1261. It staggered on in a crippled state until 1453. The resentment of the dreadful deeds of 1204 remains strongly felt in Orthodoxy, and is still directed at the office which sent the crusade eastwards (if not to them), the Papacy.

Orthodoxy thought and thinks of the church as governed by councils, with no single person in any office controlling the whole church; the Catholic West, however, was moving in a different direction. Rome was not the first city in which the office of bishop was developed. Indeed, to begin with, the church in Rome appears to have been governed by a group of leaders acting together. That soon changed, however, and the Bishop of Rome soon became a person of significance not only within the Christian community of Rome but within the wider company of the bishops of the various towns which had churches. When the emperor moved to Constantinople, the Bishop of Rome soon filled the space of leadership, especially in times of threat and harassment as the emperor in far-off Constantinople had less and less real power in Italy and the Germanic invaders were making their way south. If a comparison is made between the Pope in Rome and the Patriarch in Constantinople, we may see the office developing in these places in continuity with the previous culture of the place: for Rome, the legal administration of the empire, for Constantinople, the style of church leaders, although in both places, doubtless, ethnic and genetic features must have contributed to the culture. We can also see the emperor's presence in one city as a channel for keeping the patriarch in a decidedly secondary place, while the emperor's absence from Rome eases the pope's rise to pre-eminence, indeed, even makes it necessary.

Rome was a special place for Christian people because Peter and Paul had died there, both, it was believed, martyrs for their faith. The graves of saints provided a very strong reason for regarding that town as especially holy and significant. And twentyfirst-century readers need to pause and consider something of the atmosphere of belief represented by that claim. Had Peter been no different from the other eleven of Jesus' twelve disciples the fact that he and the great Apostle Paul were buried in Rome would have given the Church of Rome great status. But Peter was seen as the leader of the disciples after the death of Jesus; and, more powerfully, Peter's leadership is expressed in St Matthew's Gospel in association with the church and its author-ity to forgive sins. Some say the verse applies to the whole church, and not exclusively to Peter. But from early times many believed that either it applied to Peter alone or that its application to the whole church included the church's working with, through and under Peter's leadership. If Peter is held to be the first Bishop of Rome and if you believe that the authority given to Peter by Jesus was transmitted through the succession of Bishops of Rome, one after another, you are then in a position to claim that each pope is called by God to lead the whole church, that is, the entire company of Christian people throughout the world. If the argument is accepted this far, it remains for some specificity to be added to the claim; just what exactly should the leadership of the pope be?

Two popes by the name of Gregory did much to spell out the answer. The first Gregory became Pope at the end of the sixth century, the first monk to hold the office. He came from a wealthy family, was trained as a lawyer, and had held office as Prefect, the chief citizen of Rome. He brought to the papal office the assurance and skill which he possessed, as well as a devout piety and concern for contemplation. The office of pope grew in stature and authority through him. He became known as Gregory the Great. He is also known for his concern for mission, sending Augustine to England and encouraging the continued use for Christian worship of buildings and sites that had been sacred in pre-Christian times. The other Gregory was Pope Gregory VII, who was pope in the eleventh century. His reform of the office gave the pope new power. All bishops were required to swear allegiance to him. With considerable lands in Italy and great wealth each pope became a ruler of great power in matters other than what might be called religious (though making a distinction between religious and other aspects of life is more expressive of our twentyfirst-century world than it was of the world of either Gregory). It should be said that the increase in papal power was not entirely an advance made by Rome against unwilling church people across Europe. Many were looking for guidance; there was need for consistency and common standards; and Western Europe was lacking in political leadership able to bring peace and promote civilised ways of living.

The Church of Constantinople, with its wonderful Great Church of Sancta Sophia (later a mosque, now a museum, but still there) continued its glorious liturgies. Hemmed in by the Muslim world to its south and east, and the Catholic world to the west, it looked north, and the ways of Orthodoxy became the form of Christianity adopted by Russia. As Constantinople declined, Moscow increased. The former had spoken of itself as the Second Rome, or New Rome; the latter took up the title of Third Rome. The Czars, after all, were Caesars.

Searching for Better Ways

The story of Saint Francis of Assisi has never ceased to have wide appeal. He has often been called 'the second Christ' and was so designated (*alter Christus*) by Pope Pius XI in 1926. He was born Giovanni di Bernadone in Assisi, Italy, in 1181 or 1182. His family were successful merchants, and he intended to become a knight in arms. Instead, he underwent a deep conversion, attracted deeply by Christ, and drawn to the character of the historical Jesus as he is presented in the New Testament Gospels. The point needs to be emphasised, if we are to appreciate Francis' significance, that without rejecting or diminishing the belief that Jesus was divine, he wished people to admire and follow the humanity of Jesus as an example and pattern for their lives. Christ had been regarded as throned in glory. Even on his cross he was depicted crowned and robed in splendour. Francis wanted people to recognise their Lord as a poor man who desired his followers to share his poverty by giving up unnecessary possessions. He gathered round him a small band of people who accepted his vision, and obtained the permission of Pope Innocent III – a pope of great ability and achievement – to found an order. They were not to be monks, living together in a place apart, but serving people in the towns where they lived, while also taking time, as Francis himself did, to retreat into quiet places to think and pray, and, most especially, to commune with nature and derive knowledge and inspiration from plants, animals and birds, and from the sun, the moon and the stars. The hymn 'All creatures of our God and King', which is translated from words attributed to Francis, expresses that celebration of the natural world which was so important to him.

Francis's emphasis on nature and human nature had an influence in the developments in painting which flourished in Italy in the centuries after his life. The work of the painter Giotto, including his paintings of the life of Francis, shows a new ability to depict people in characterful detail and to record the landscape with equal descriptive precision. The artistic developments of the thirteenth century and onwards will always feature strongly in the story of Christianity. France, England, Germany, the Netherlands and northern Italy saw a rapid increase in trade and wealth in the thirteenth century which brought about a huge increase in building, including the erection of a vast number of churches in the

Gothic style. The great cathedrals continue to this day to fill the visitor with wonder and excitement, and with admiration for the vision, skill, and enormous labour that went into them. The paintings of Piero della Francesca and Fra Angelico in the fifteenth century, and of Leonardo da Vinci, Raphael and Botticelli later in the same century are inseparable in their brilliance from the themes, especially of Christ and Mary, which tie them to the Christian religion. El Greco uniquely combined the Greek icon-painting background of his native Crete with the skills of the Venetians (who ruled Crete) in drawing and colour. In the late sixteenth century the wonderfully detailed, descriptive work of Caravaggio led to the powerful ways in which biblical themes were expressed by Velasquez and Rembrandt. When westerners of the twenty-first century are drawn to great paintings of Christ and Mary, or when they gather in crowds to listen to a Bach Mass, while professing no Christian conviction or engaging in any recognisable form of religious practice, the questions which arise in the mind of a member of the clergy may include asking how greatly the churches of modern times have failed to incorporate the work of artists in their acts of worship. Yet such questions may be both pretentious and pointless. It is possible that a person whose mind freezes when invited by a priest to pray may come across a prayer written by, say, Samuel Johnson, and find that the words express something deep and true, and be enriched by them, to the extent that they bring some needed balance and enlargement of hope – which is what the poor priest may have hoped for when he uttered the freezing words 'Let us pray'.

One important element in understanding Christianity, which is connected to what has been said about art, is the place of festivals; and Francis' contribution to the keeping of Christmas fits well with the rest of his great legacy. Christmas had developed as a festival much later than Easter, Pentecost, or Epiphany. Francis kept Christmas with great enthusiasm. It fitted his desire to remind people of the humanity of Christ. On Christmas Eve in 1223 he preached at Midnight Mass with a manger which he had arranged to be placed in the church, together with animals. It was the first Christmas crib or crèche, and to that extent we may say that Francis invented the popular Christmas, since the manger scene is multiplied a million times on cards and public displays, as well as acting as a visual reminder of the scene from St Luke's Gospel, where Mary is said to have laid the child Jesus in a manger 'because there was no room for them in the inn'. (The image of the manger was probably used by Luke because of the verse in the Prophecy of Isaiah in which the prophet presents God saying that the ox and the ass know where their food is to be found, but his people have forgotten to seek their nourishment from him.)

How often should Christian people go to church? Although in the lifetime of Saint Paul most members possibly attended every week, unless they were unable to do so, the time must have come fairly early in the life of the church when some people were less frequently at worship than others. The Fourth Lateran Council of 1215 instructed that everybody should receive communion at least once a year, and that minimum requirement became the norm by the end of the Middle Ages, though people might be often present at church services without participating in the Eucharist. For many centuries, in most parts of the Christian Church, there have been some people who went to church most Sundays, while others attended on great occasions like Christmas and Easter or took part in popular processions on feast days honouring a local saint or Mary, when the atmosphere must often have been a mixture of solemnity and carnival, ordered ritual and mass movement. In some places, including Spain and Latin America, such occasions continue to happen. In other places, community celebration with a Christian foundation may be held to be improper or impracticable in the context of a multicultural society and one where religion is regarded as a personal option and not an instrument of social cohesion. It is worth asking if the rhythm of great festive occasions breaking up a weekly pattern contains something deeply valuable, and also whether there is, in the churches, too simplistic an assumption that the people who are present every week are superior Christians to those who attend more infrequently – or, even if they know that it does not sound well to regard themselves as superior, nevertheless it is accepted that they are entitled to determine the policies and shape the action of the churches. As should be well known, there are many reasons for being in church frequently, and many for being present infrequently, or not at all.

Francis' devotion to the humanity of Christ led not only to his enriching the imagery of the celebration of his birth at Christmas, but also to a deep attachment to his death on the cross. In September 1224 he had been meditating for forty days in a quiet place in the hills between Arezzo and Florence, when he saw a vision of Christ on the cross. It is said that the experience was powerfully intense, and that Francis then experienced nail-holes forming in his hands and feet, where the holes of nails had pierced the hands and feet of Jesus. These marks are called stigmata, which is the Greek word for 'marks', in the statement by Saint Paul in his Epistle to the Galatians that 'I bear in my body the marks of the Lord Jesus' (Galatians 6: 17). The phenomenon of stigmatisation is one which has been reported hundreds of times since the days of Francis. It is not an easy one for modern minds to accept. It is, however, part of the Christian story – and it prevents modern westerners from regarding the saint of Assisi as an ecological humanitarian with a sentimental approach to Christmas.

Francis' Order of Friars Minor ('lesser brothers') grew in numbers rapidly. Ten years after seeking the pope's approval in 1210, Francis could count five thousand Franciscans, devoted to poverty and care, and to preaching (not doctrine, but penance). In 1212 a woman of similar privileged background to Francis', Clare, founded an order for women. The Poor Clares, like the Friars Minor, took vows of poverty, chastity, and obedience. The Franciscans have made a huge contribution to the life and work of the church, though some members have challenged the church's ownership of property and money beyond what was acceptable to Rome. Consistent idealists can be a source of discomfort to any institution.

Another order, the Order of Preachers, was founded soon after the Franciscans. It is more commonly called the Dominican Order, named after the founder, Dominic, a Spanish monk. They were formed out of a group of preachers whom Dominic had led in reaction to the Cathars, a group of deeply committed people who, in the years around 1200, in some places rivalled the Catholic Church, with large numbers, and their own bishops, tolerated and sometimes supported by local princes. Their name comes from the Greek word *katharos*, meaning 'pure' (the source of the name Katharine). They carried to extreme that element in Christian thought which suspects matter and the flesh, to the extent that they rejected the notion of God becoming human, or of the God-man being crucified. They were opposed to sexual intercourse and Holy Communion, both having too much to do with matter as distinct from spirit. In 1209 an army of northern French barons and bishops carried out a bloody siege and fight against the Cathars in Beziers and Carcassone in Languedoc. It was not a good example of how the established Church ought best to react to divergence of opinion. Dominic's approach was to preach and teach, and his order, spreading widely across Europe, became dedicated to education. They were also used to seek out heresy, in a process of questioning (the word for the questioning, inquisition, becoming rather notorious over the centuries). When Spanish and Portuguese explorers began these nations' empires in the New World, after Columbus' Atlantic crossing of 1492 and Vasco da Gama's rounding of the Cape of Good Hope in 1497, Dominican priests were often there, seeking to convert the inhabitants to Christian commitment.

It is not surprising that the Cathar movement should have provoked the opposition of the Church, especially since their large numbers matched the unacceptable nature of their ideas. Another group, however, whose origins appear to have much in common with those of the Franciscans, met with considerable hostility from the Church, including persecution to the point of death. The Waldensians are a group, now in Italy, whose foundation followed the decision of a rich French merchant, Peter Waldo, to give away his wealth and live a life of poverty. With a few followers, he started preaching to people around Lyon where he lived. In his desire to share the teaching of Jesus with his hearers, he had translations made from the Bible into vernacular French. They petitioned Rome to be recognised, but the Third Lateran Council of 1179 rejected their request. Subsequently, they were banned from preaching. They continued nevertheless, and developed new and threatening practices, including permitting women to preach. One can appreciate that the Church found it unacceptable that a group should feel free to preach without official church approval, and also that the innovative practice of reading the Bible in the languages of everyday conversation threatened the Church's control of what parts of the Bible were to be exposed, and what interpretation made of them. But the huge distinction between the responses, respectively, to Francis and Peter Waldo, men apparently of similar motivation, may depend on the style the two men and their groups adopted, as well as on the nature of their requests and activities. Francis was a conciliator. When forbidden to preach by a bishop in his area, he went away, returning later to make the request again, when it was granted. There is no doubt also, without any prejudice against Waldo, that Francis was a man of enormous charm and personal appeal. Yet the fear which could enter the mind of a senior churchman at the thought of people hearing the Bible in their own tongues was very great.

Waldo was not the only person seeking the Bible in the vernacular, and Francis, Clare, and Dominic were not the only people seeking new commitment and deepening of spiritual awareness, as well as better teaching and devotion to the needs of poor people. Here and there, in the new universities of Paris, Oxford, Bologna and other places, minds were continuing to grapple with old problems. The classical writers of ancient Greece and Rome were being studied again, thanks in part to the scholarship of the Muslim world which had protected these writings and studied them when they were lost to Christian Europe. And the invention of the printing press meant that thoughts could spread like wildfire.

The Church's New Formations

The twentieth-century theologian Paul Tillich put forward the idea that the words 'Catholic' and 'Protestant', as well as referring to the Roman Catholic Church and such others as the Methodists, Baptists, Church of England, and Lutherans, might be usefully used to indicate two aspects of the whole Christian Church, or of any part of it – any church – which a church, to be good and Christian, should possess. The Catholic aspect is the continuity of believing and practising from the days of the first Apostles, with a sense of corporate mutual support and organisational cohesion. The Protestant element is the bringing of critical examination, at any time, by individuals and groups to the official corporate view, with the right to deviate from the majority, and the official majority's duty to pay attention to critics and reformers. Possibly most churches would now wish to be both Catholic and Protestant in the sense just offered of the terms. The Roman Catholic Church includes many who would wish for their church the continuous possibility of reform, while churches whose forebears might have regarded the word Catholic as a term almost of abuse would wish to be Catholic both in their faithfulness to essential Christianity and in having a well-ordered set of arrangements for working together as a community. When we consider the ways in which, in the sixteenth century, northern Europe saw established churches, part of the system centred on Rome and 'under' the pope, become churches which had broken that Rome connection and organised themselves differently, occupying the same church buildings as before and being generally regarded as the sole churches of their areas, with little opportunity given to individual members to speak out against the official view or propose significant innovations, we might well regard these churches as more Catholic than Protestant, in Tillich's sense of the terms. Such a point may be especially helpful in view of any assumption or conviction that the changes in these churches (the changes which tend to be known collectively as the Reformation) represented a huge transition from imposed religion to religion based on private judgement, from a world in which church authorities told people what to believe to a world in which people made up their own minds about truth and standards, and opted for the church of their choice almost, but not entirely, like opting for a shoe shop or newspaper shop selected from a large local provision of both. It was not like that. Calvin's Geneva was not a free-for-all.

'Everyone' knows that the name Martin Luther is associated, more than any other, with the Reformation in Germany. The question is often asked, 'How essential was Luther to the changes in the church?' Would they have happened without him? To what extent did the events involving Luther trigger off comparable events in Switzerland, France, and elsewhere? There is no doubt that princes and other powerful people were becoming weary of the monarchical papacy; that there was a widespread interest in having the Bible in the languages of ordinary speech; and a desire to recover the original meaning, thrust and air of the New Testament accompanied the restored study of the writings of classical Greece and Rome. But general trends require specific instances. Luther was highly specific, a man of character and colour, emotional, gifted, strong. A miner's son, he was monk, priest, and university professor, remaining the last of these until his death.

He was born in 1483 and became a monk in 1505. His reason for doing so will say something about him as well as about the time in which he lived. Caught in a thunderstorm the student Luther vowed to Saint Anne, the Virgin Mary's mother, that if he escaped he would become a monk, and he did. In 1507 he was ordained priest and found the mass a terrifying and humbling experience – that he should be in the presence of the divine Christ there in the sacramental host. In 1511 he became Professor of Scripture at the recently founded University of Wittenberg, and in 1515 he was also given authority over eleven monasteries of his Augustinian order. His study of the Bible, and especially of the Epistle to the Romans, convinced him that his frenzied attempts to win the favour of God by fulfilling many ritual duties and engaging in acts of penance and self-mortification were not only unnecessary but pointless; that the favour of God is given freely, his grace to all who have faith in him; and that the assurance of that grace by that faith is given through the Bible. Luther therefore made these three the great principles and slogans of his life, thought, and church leadership: *Sola scriptura, sola gratia, sola fides* – salvation, the right relationship with God, received according to scripture, by grace, through faith. That these emphases interpret the epistle well may not be doubted. That they are for many a summary of basic Christianity can readily be accepted. What is also important is that they came as release and light to one whose guilt-ridden anxiety about his relationship with God was crying out for help and liberation.

As he developed his new focus on the meaning of the Christian Gospel, he found himself having increasing doubts about much of the ritual and administrative life of the church of which he was a priest. Acts of penance and pilgrimages to shrines he rejected in that he could not any longer accept that these acts were ways of ensuring, buying even, the grace and kindness of God (though others have gone on pilgrimages as aids to faith without any sense of purchasing divine favour). He made his first public challenge on a matter which might be regarded as having little to defend it, even in the minds of those who supported other traditions such as pilgrimages. The matter was the sale of indulgences, whereby a person could give money to the church and in return be assured that not only would you be excused paying whatever penalty had been imposed for some sin you had committed, but that even after you died the money would free you from periods of purgatory. The sale of indulgences which provoked Luther's protest was made, in part, to provide finance for building work the pope intended in Rome, including St Peter's Basilica (over the shrine of Saint Peter, the symbol and basis of papal position and power). When Johann Tetzel, a Dominican theologian, preached a sermon supporting the indulgence sale, Luther responded in an accepted scholarly way, by writing some points for debate and fixing them to the door of the Castle church in Wittenberg. There were ninety five points, called theses, and the date was 31 October 1517.

The challenge was taken up by Rome. Luther was given repeated opportunities to recant, and refused. He wrote prolifically, expanding his criticism of the Church as it existed from indulgences to the papacy, clerical celibacy, sacraments (apart from baptism and the Eucharist), masses for the dead, religious orders of monks and friars, and other Catholic practices and institutions. He received the protection of the Elector Frederick of Saxony who kept him in seclusion for a period for his safety. The Church banned his books and he was excommunicated. At the same time there appeared in towns and cities others who promoted radical reform of religion, and an emphasis on the Gospel of Christ, faithful to Saint Paul's expression and interpretation of it. Luther gave up wearing his monk's habit, and he married a former Cistercian nun, Catherine von Bora. All this was done by 1525, a mere eight years after the Wittenberg theses.

Martin Luther was a man of great gifts, one being his power of communication and skill with words. His writings were printed, and they spread and were read rapidly and widely. One thousand of his sermons have been preserved, as well as his pamphlets and other works. Chief among his writing, however, is his translation of the Bible into German. In it he employed creative brilliance and used phrases and images from common life to produce a Bible of great warmth and beauty, which has remained a great treasure of the

Lutheran churches and of the German language. His New Testament went through one hundred separate editions in his own lifetime. He has been called the greatest sculptor of the German language, and his Bible played a large part in the development of modern German. His concern that Jesus and the Gospel be presented in human terms, reminiscent of Francis of Assisi, was exemplified when he criticised mediaeval paintings of the Virgin Mary for presenting Mary as flawlessly beautiful, with nothing to suggest that she was an ordinary young woman.

He loved beauty, and he stands out among the reformers for his defence of traditional crucifixes and other religious works of art in churches. He did not see why refusal to worship or adore them as objects worthy of such veneration prevent people using them as aids to worship. He also did much to promote church music, and his hymns won him much popular admiration and support. Some reformers believed that only the psalms in the Bible should be sung by worshipping congregations, and there are some churches where the psalms remain the only words sung; but Luther's hymns and the subsequent hymns and chorales of other poets and composers have enriched the lives of Lutheran congregations. One of the finest examples of the union of words and music is in the Passions, according to St Matthew and St John, of Johann Sebastian Bach (1685-1750), using the words of Luther's Bible to tell of Christ's passion and crucifixion. We might note the important part played in other languages by translations of the Bible, including the English translation of 1611, known in Britain in the past as the Authorised Version and now widely called the King James Bible – even sometimes the Saint James Bible, presumably because 'saint' sounds holier than 'king'. It has been said that it was no accident that the 1611 Bible was translated at the time when Shakespeare was writing. The rhythms and cadences of that version coloured the speech of English speakers for centuries, and communicated mystery and wonder to the hearers.

The movement for reform was, in the days of the first Apostles, advanced in towns rather than in the rural areas, despite the division of the population between town and country being much less dominated by the urban areas than in recent times. (The question may be put, of how far churches have based their way of doing things on urban situations, and then tried to impose these ways on the people of the countryside.) Luther was caught up in conflict emerging from the rural peasantry which pushed him to express views not only on the matter in question but on the relevance of the Gospel to political matters. The Peasants' Revolt of 1524 – 25 saw rural workers latch on to Luther's criticisms of the prevailing church situation, and demand better conditions, more freedom, and higher pay. Luther stressed that he was not calling for a general revolution, that the Gospel promised a spiritual kingdom and not an earthly or political paradise. Inequality was inevitable in human affairs. He went so far as to say that anyone who killed a rebellious peasant was doing a service to God. The German princes suppressed the revolt, and over one hundred thousand peasants were killed. Luther's speech was often expressed in strong terms, which pleased his admirers and gave fuel to his enemies. He also found his belief that the Christian Church had replaced Judaism leading him to write in an anti-Semitic way which stands in a long line of statements, before and since. Near the end of his life, he advocated burning Jewish homes and expelling all Jews from Germany. It does not make pleasant reading, especially for those who admire much of his character and achievement. He had strong confidence in the rights and powers of princes, magistrates, and civil authorities, holding that the spiritual kingdom of God and the civil kingdom were distinct, but leaving much of the authority over the church to these civil governors. It left a close connection of church and state in Germany and Scandinavia which may have brought the benefit of holding communities together after the model of Christendom, while encouraging a rather uncritical attitude of church to rulers.

Things were different in Geneva, where the French lawyer John Calvin (1509 – 64) took the lead in developing what was already a city of reformation, in that the magistrates had decided to take steps to remove the authority of Rome in their town. Calvin's authority was considerable, although he was absent from the city for a period of years following a dispute with the magistrates. He was far more interested than Luther was in the details of church organisation and discipline. It has been said that one of the ways in which his Scottish disciple, John Knox, differed from him concerned the extent to which a congregation needed to be established in good order before Holy Communion could be held there. If Calvin acted on the judgement that the administration of the sacrament should follow the 'proper' establishment of church order, Knox, it is argued, tended to the view that the church did not make the sacrament as much as the sacrament made the church – that instead of waiting until the right arrangements were in place before a Communion service could be held, the holding of such a service itself brought the church into being in that place. It is an interesting point to ponder. Some will say that common sense points in the direction of getting some sort of orderly arrangement in place, with people knowing who they are and why they are there, before you hold the chief ritual event which expresses and celebrates the heart of your organisation and its function and purpose. Yet the other way of seeing it will also seem to have truth in it – that being gathered round the bread and wine and the actions and words which compose the Eucharist brings Christian people in response to an invitation to find themselves formed into a company, a part of the church, in fact to become the church in a way which is deeper than just joining an organisation because you choose to do so, on the grounds that you agree with its official position. It is, however, one thing to report Calvin's concern for good order in the church. It would be quite another thing, and absurdly inaccurate, to conclude from that concern that he regarded church membership as coming from the decision and judgement of the member, rather than from the initiative and grace of God. He stood solidly in the line of Paul and Augustine, emphasising the central significance of divine grace. He also provided the single most substantial scholarly writing of the Reformation in his *Institutes of the Christian Religion*, in which the central place of the Bible in Christian thought is affirmed, together with his recognition of the value of paying attention to the insights of those who worked on the meaning and significance of Christ and the Trinity in the early Christian centuries.

Sixteenth-century Europe now saw a major shift in church authority and organisation, as well as in doctrine and forms of worship. Roughly, there were three sorts: (1) those who remained connected to Rome, continuing the Catholic Church (of the west, as distanced from the Orthodox in the east) – largely the countries on the north shore of the Mediterranean from the Iberian peninsula (Portugal and Spain) through France (less united) to Italy, and also Bavaria and Poland (the Catholic Church came to be known as the Roman Catholic Church, since the churches of the Reformation considered themselves to be part of the Catholic Church); (2) Lutheran churches, in much of Germany, as well as Denmark and Sweden (then comprising all Scandinavia); and (3) Reformed churches, in Switzerland, Bohemia, the Netherlands and Scotland, as well as parts of Germany and Hungary. England at that time contained elements in common with the Reformed group. It may be noted that the name 'Lutheran' appears to have been adopted early, and without controversy. The Reformed churches, however, were never officially called 'Calvinist', and indeed the word was used principally as a term of abuse. Calvin's Geneva became influential in other places, notably in Scotland, where the leading reformer, John Knox, brought to his homeland his experience and admiration of the way the Swiss city, massively influenced by Calvin, arranged matters of church and state, legally enforcing the keeping of Sunday as the Sabbath, prohibiting gambling, dancing, extravagant dress, going to theatres and taverns, and making heresy punishable by death (the last put into practice notoriously when Servetus, a Spaniard, was burned for denying the doctrine of the Trinity). The Church of Scotland, which adopted the Presbyterian form of church government over the next century, showed some of the same fervour for simplicity that marked Geneva, and even today it is possible to raise a laugh by making the suggestion that 'Presbyterians' are mean-spirited, censorious, and deeply suspicious of pleasure.

The best-known fact about the Reformation in England is that King Henry VIII broke the link between the English church and the papacy because the pope refused to annul the king's marriage, which would allow him to re-marry in the hope of obtaining a male heir. In those times, marriage and child-bearing were matters of politics, as indeed were papal annulments (the pope's refusal having much to do with the king's wife being the aunt of Charles V who had a considerable military hold on Rome). The winds of Luther's ideas and other continental ideas had been blowing in England, however, and, in addition, the higher clergy were extremely unpopular. The Reformation Parliament of 1529 – 36 gave the king his divorce, and made him Supreme Head of the Church, with power to define doctrine. Reform of the clergy was ordered, and the monasteries were confiscated. Soon an English translation of the Bible, a revision of Tyndale's first English Bible, was put into the churches. The Prayer Book of Archbishop Thomas Cranmer brought together Catholic and Lutheran prayers, as well as those of the compiler, in a book which has been loved by English speakers ever since and made a great contribution to the culture of the English-speaking world. Influences from both Luther's Germany and Calvin's Geneva sought to affect the development of the English church. Under Henry's successor, Edward VI, the direction was Reformed (taking a clearly hostile view of anything with a whiff of transubstantiation, for example); but, after the short reign of the Catholic Queen Mary, Elizabeth's long reign saw the Church of England become more definitively 'Anglican', with the Queen now as Supreme Governor (rather than Head), and the liturgy unspecific enough to allow more than one view (or none) on the definition of 'Presence' in the Eucharist.

These new formations represent one side of the events and changes commonly called the Reformation. The other side is the new order and energy in the (Roman) Catholic Church, represented by the Council of Trent and the involvement of the church in the imperial conquests of Spain and Portugal.

A Wider, Deeper Catholicism

Ignatius of Loyola was born in his ancestral castle of Loyola in the last decade of the fifteenth century, the same decade in which two sea voyages burst the western boundaries of Europe and led to consequences for the Christian Church which, at the beginning of the twenty-first century, have yet to make their greatest impact. Ignatius, the founder of the Jesuits (the Society of Jesus), may represent the deepening of spiritual life in the century after Luther and the Reformation. The two voyagers, Columbus and Vasco da Gama, may stand for the thirst for new trade routes when the way to the east was blocked by the Muslim Empire. Both movements, however, the spiritual and the geographical, can be considered together, both in their causes and in their practice. There was a new thrusting energy in sixteenth-century Europe, an increased emphasis on the individual, a robust effort to promote a more faithful Christianity in both Catholic and Protestant communities, and such enthusiasm and initiative may be said to colour both the deepening of the spiritual life represented by Ignatius and the mixture of exploitation and mission which featured in the expanding empires, initially of Spain and Portugal. In 1492 Christopher Columbus, a native of Genoa, crossed the Atlantic, sponsored by King Ferdinand and Queen Isabella of Spain, in search of a western route to India, and found instead the islands which became known as the West Indies. Five years later Vasco de Gama set out from Portugal to seek another way to India and discovered it by sailing round Africa, returning two years later to a hero's welcome in Lisbon. Spain and Portugal, both securely Catholic in faith, thus became the first European nations to embark on the mission which was followed by others in later centuries, to win the riches of newly discovered lands and spread Christian civilisation, as they understood it, among the inhabitants of these places. As the Spanish had travelled west across the Atlantic, and the Portuguese east round the Cape of Good Hope, the pope, dividing the new territories to lessen rivalry between them, drew a line down the middle of the Atlantic Ocean. Spain was to be allowed to take over what was west of the line, and Portugal the places to the east. The fact that, after being moved further west, the line cut through the north-east corner of South America had the consequence that Brazil became part of the Portuguese Empire, with Portuguese as the language of Brazil, while most of the rest of the continent speaks Spanish. The Spanish conquered the Aztecs and the Incas of Peru. They set up stations in California, and they sailed farther westward to take the Philippines (which they could not have taken travelling east round Africa, since that would have broken the pope's dividing line). The Portuguese took territories around the coast of Africa, but chiefly they set up bases in India (Goa, on the south-west, remained Portuguese until taken by India in 1961).

Ignatius belonged to the Basque country. As a soldier, he read about Jesus and the saints while convalescing after being wounded. He went on a pilgrimage to Jerusalem, and studied in Salamanca and Paris. In 1534 he founded the Society of Jesus, and was ordained in 1537. In 1539 the society was approved by the pope. In 1622 he was canonised (that is, declared to be a saint). His *Spiritual Exercises* were deeply influential, and his rapidly growing Order played a central part both in the revitalisation of Catholic Europe and in the missionary ventures beyond the seas.

The official response of the Catholic Church to the Lutheran separation from Rome was the Council of Trent, an assembly of bishops in the Italian town of Trento. It met for the first time in 1545 and ended its last session in 1563. The fact that it began twenty-eight years after Luther's Wittenberg Theses, and took eighteen years to reach its conclusion, might suggest a certain lack of awareness of the extent of the division in the Church which Luther had inaugurated. It certainly went about its business without rush or panic, and insisted, contrary to the wishes of Emperor Charles V and other rulers, on dealing with doctrine instead of proceeding first to practical reforms. It took up points in Luther's writings and pronounced disagreement where it thought right, and it gave lengthy consideration to the doctrine of justification, the belief that sinners are by grace given righteousness. Luther claimed that the righteousness of a baptised person was the righteousness of God, 'imputed' to the individual, rather than the person's own righteousness, whereas Trent held that the baptised had righteousness of their own, with which they co-operated with the help that came from God. Is it a matter of saying much the same thing from two different perspectives? The council declared the Latin Bible of Jerome – the Vulgate – to be the official Bible of the Church, while reaching no agreement on translations into the languages which people spoke. Discipline among clergy and laity was promoted, and the authority of the pope emphasised. The Counter-Reformation stood for uniformity in doctrine and standards. It is also associated with the exuberance (or extravagance) of Baroque architecture, and with devotion to the Eucharist and the cultivation of the inner life, or personal piety. We must serve God, said Saint Ignatius, as if everything depended on ourselves; but we must pray as if all depended upon God.

The Kings of Spain and Portugal were authorised by the pope to be responsible for the spiritual care of the peoples in the new lands which came under their control. Travelling with the ships which braved the stormy seas, priests were able to act in the name of their king as well as that of the pope. Many of these priests were Jesuits, members of the Society of Jesus, but Franciscans and Dominicans also shared in the work. In both directions, west across the Atlantic and east around Africa, they went with the aim of spreading the Christian faith. Those who went east had an additional motive: they wished to make contact with fellow Christians who were believed to exist in places far away. The legend of Prester John and his Christian kingdom was widely preserved in Europe, and it is thought possible that rumours of the Ethiopian Church, so long cut off from the rest of Christendom, may lie behind it. There were also memories of travellers' tales about Christian communities in the heartland of Asia, and some did remain, though most had been overtaken by Islam, some becoming Muslims. The Church of Thomas in South India, however, was present and strong, related to the Syrian Church of Mesopotamia and receiving their bishops in succession from there. The Portuguese became determined to bring that church within the organisation of Rome, and 'united' them to the Catholic fold using methods which seem to have left little room for free decisions from the Thomas Christians – their language, for example, being hardly used in the 'discussions' which led to the union in 1599. The Church of Thomas was, however, never fully incorporated into the Roman Catholic Church, and its identity has remained, despite difficulties and divisions, until modern times.

The spread of Portuguese rule, European culture, and the Christian religion was rapid. When Francis Xavier arrived in Goa in 1542, a mere forty-four years after Vasco da Gama, he found a great city, with, we are told, as many churches and monasteries as could be found in a southern European city. Xavier was one of the first companions of Ignatius, and he became one of the most famous of all Christian missionaries. Like Ignatius he was a Basque. They both exemplified the Jesuit self-discipline, utter dedication to their task, and total obedience to the pope. Teachers and persuaders, diplomats and scholars, they and their fellow Jesuits were concerned with teaching and preaching, with special eagerness to influence the leaders of communities and nations, both in old Europe and in the new territories. In India, therefore, Xavier was devoted to the teaching of Christian doctrine, albeit in the most straightforward form, to people who had been led to Christian baptism with little, if any, preparation. He had translations made into Tamil of the Lord's Prayer, the Creed, and the Ten Commandments, which were not very good translations, but accurate in parts.

The Jesuits in India had good relations with the Mughal (Mogul) rulers who came to power as the Portuguese were developing their base in Goa. The great King Akbar sought out Christian missionaries to learn from them about their religion, and showed them intelligent courtesy, a reflection of his tolerant religious stance to the mainly Hindu population over which he ruled. The Mughals, who were Muslim, ruled over a largely united India from the middle of the sixteenth century until the rise of British rule in the nineteenth. As in the Ottoman Empire of the eastern Mediterranean, and in mediaeval Spain, Muslim rulers in India demonstrated a respect for other religions that many Christians would have done well to emulate.

The urge to spread Christianity took Jesuit missionaries to Japan and China in the sixteenth and early seventeenth centuries. People in Europe at that time had only the sketchiest knowledge of Japan, but Francis Xavier was keen to go there, and arrived in 1549, setting out immediately to try to express Christian ideas in the Japanese language. He remained for twenty-seven months, and died in 1552 on an island within sight of mainland China, which he had greatly desired to visit. The work he began in Japan continued over the next half-century, and was notable both for conversions to Christianity, numbered in tens of thousands, and for the respect and diplomatic skill which leading missionaries showed towards the Japanese people and culture. Xavier and his successors were full of admiration for the highly developed style of Japanese life, and the willingness of people to consider ideas which were new to them. It helped that Buddhism at the time was not highly regarded among the people, and was at low ebb. One of the significant instances of clever respect for local customs was in the choice of what material the missionaries should wear. The choice was cotton or silk, that is, the clothes of the poor or the clothes of the rulers. The Superior of the Mission argued that it was appropriate for Christian missionaries to be poor and to dress as poor people, but he was overruled by the powerful Alessandro Valignano, an Italian Jesuit sent from Rome with powers to visit the missions in the east. He took the view that the missionaries must wear silk in order to be welcome among the rich aristocracy, and his decision bore fruit. He was also keen that there be ordinations of Japanese converts to the priesthood, but few were ordained, despite quite a number studying Christian theology. The church in Japan, brought into being in this careful, diplomatic way, soon suffered enormous persecution from local rulers, and it was swept from the scene for two centuries. What Xavier and others had shown was a willingness to encourage Christian belief and practice without disparaging or destroying the indigenous culture of Japan. That respect was dependent on the judgement that existing Japanese culture was sufficiently developed and acceptable to be treated in that way.

Many other places and their indigenous culture did not meet these European yardsticks, though the local heritage often had its own way of remaining in the background, even when the missionaries may have thought they had destroyed it; and in some situations the merging of pre-Christian ritual and symbol with overtly Christian examples is clear and plain to see, as in Latin America.

In China the Jesuits showed their subtle appreciation of local culture, finding it acceptable to revere ancestors, and to continue offering ritual respect to Confucius. Led by Matteo Ricci, they were welcomed into the imperial household in Beijing, and their sharing of as much local culture as was possible brought about a Chinese church, with small congregations in several parts of this huge country. They encountered occasional hostility, but their chief obstacle was the growing insistence from Rome that the Catholic Church be uniform, the same in every place, with Latin used in services rather than local languages, and a ban put on Christians participating in such ceremonies as the veneration of ancestors in China. It is only possible to speculate, without any certainty, what might have happened if the attitudes to local culture shown in Japan and China, with the use of the vernacular, had been allowed to develop throughout the world. The Jesuits incurred the hostility of other orders for their concentration on approaches to the aristocracy, and their influence and methods brought about widespread opposition, with the result that the society was suppressed between 1773 and 1814, though it continued to operate at a reduced level during that period.

When the Spanish sailed west from their new lands in America to take the islands of the Philippines, they met no highly developed civilisation, and as a result they bequeathed a devotion to the Christian religion which has left the Philippines as the only Christian nation of the East. The principal Spanish territories, however, were in Central and South America, taken over remarkably soon after Columbus' 1492 discovery. Under Cortes they took over the lands of the Aztecs in Mexico, and under Pizarro they made Peru of the Incas Spanish. They also conquered the Mayan lands of Yucatan, Chiapas and Guatemala. Similarities to Christian symbols and rites were noticed in the complicated religious practices of these peoples, and elements were more or less unofficially blended together – notably in the veneration of the Virgin Mary with the local Mother Goddess in the background. Great churches were soon built, and a parish system developed. It all led to the present-day situation where a high proportion of the world's Christians – and even more of the world's Catholics – live in the Americas south of the Rio Grande.

Entering the Modern World

There have probably been people at all times who have taken the view that events in history occur according to a fixed plan, ordained by God, or by fate, and that they could not possibly have happened otherwise. Such a view is to be distinguished from an inclination to find a propitious development in a chain of events, a happy outcome from a series of happenings, some of which may have been painful. That second position does not depend on there being a fixed arrangement with no possibility of deviation or alternatives. You can detect a set of links between one event and another, leading to a situation which you regard as good, and still recognise that things might have been otherwise, even to the extent that another chain of events might have produced an even happier present situation. There is much to be said for looking to the past and feeling grateful, without looking to the future and feeling trapped.

As the sixteenth century gave way to the seventeenth, a mixture of attitudes to the extent to which events are pre-ordained can be found. The ethos of much of post-Reformation Europe was one of openness to developing trade and commerce, and also of liberty to look at traditional beliefs with fresh critical scholarship. At the same time there were many instances of authoritarian religion, with punitive action taken against those who dared to express independent or 'heretical' opinions. Those parts of the church which were influenced by John Calvin maintained both a strong attachment to the doctrine of an active, controlling God and an adherence to strict church discipline in which leaders exercised control over the conduct, as well as the beliefs, of church members.

The recognition that things might have been other than they were can lead both to a feeling of the accidental character of human events and to a sense that there must have been some divine purpose in a chain of happenings so loosely held together. If someone with the strength and genius of Martin Luther had not been active in the first quarter of the sixteenth century, might the Church have kept its unity, in a reformed, and less centrally organised way. If, at the end of the previous century, the 'Catholic Sovereigns' Ferdinand and Isabella had not triumphed over the Muslims in Spain, might the expansion of Spanish power to the Americas have been Islamic rather than Christian? If the religious life in the territory which became the United States of America had been led by representatives of one united church, what effect might that have had on the cultural and economic (and therefore military) development of that country, both in itself and as a world power? Such questions can kindle the imagination, and give food for thought both to those who wish to see a pattern of divine providence in human affairs and to those who are quite sceptical about it.

The first English colonies on the North American mainland in the seventeenth century certainly brought to the beginnings of Christianity in the United States that transitional combination of church discipline and individual liberty, especially in the New England area (the first colony, in Virginia, being more loosely organised religiously, and more like the broad church parishes of the Church of England, which indeed they were). Puritan leaders of the Massachusetts Bay Colony saw themselves leading a people with a special relationship to God, called by him to be like the ancient Israelites, enjoying divine favour when they followed his rules, and interpreting hardship as his punishment for their disobedience. Their first governor, John Winthrop, told the settlers, 'We must consider that we shall be as a City upon a Hill. The eyes of all people are upon us.' Later in the seventeenth century, a Puritan theologian wrote: 'We are as a city set upon a hill, in open view of all the earth, the eyes of the world are upon us, because we profess ourselves to be a people in covenant with God, and therefore not only the Lord our God, with whom we have made covenant, but heaven and earth, angels and men, that are witness to our profession, will cry shame upon us if we walk contrary to the covenant which we have professed and promised to walk in.' [Peter Bulkeley, The Gospel Covenant: or the Covenant of the Grace Opened 1651, in *The Annals of America*, Vol. 1 (Chicago 1968), p212.] The theme of the deep significance of the new beginning across the Atlantic remained prominent in New England, and it would not be fanciful to trace that sense of destiny and world prominence, with and without religious language, in the later development of the United States.

Land was plentiful in North America. There were, of course, indigenous inhabitants, the descendants of those who had crossed from Siberia in ancient times, when crossing by land was possible. In the sixteenth century there were probably about one million native Americans, in many tribes, with developed rituals and languages, often at war with one another, some quietly peaceful, and others more belligerent. The behaviour of the new European settlers to them varied, though they were rarely respectful of their cultural heritage. The thirst for religious freedom led to new settlers finding new land in which they could live freely, with Baptists, who were opposed to the baptism of babies, finding a home in Rhode Island, and Quakers settling there and, most notably, in Pennsylvania, where William Penn was granted the land by King Charles II in 1681. The Quakers, or Society of Friends, had been founded by George Fox, an Englishman who, in the seventeenth century, rejected the churches as they were, and promoted the view that any person could have a direct relationship with God. 'When all my hopes in them [the churches] and in all men were gone,' he said, 'I heard a voice which said, "There is one, even Christ Jesus, that can speak to thy condition."' Rejecting the need for creeds or doctrines, members of the Society met for worship without set liturgies, speaking as they were moved. All members were able to participate, and, notably in those early times, women had full equality with men.

Christian religion was moving from public duty to private feeling. The two are not mutually exclusive. One can follow the rules of an established church and do so gladly and willingly; and one can regard the individual's relationship to God as paramount while treating the association of fellow believers for worship and support as important too. The trend, however, was in the direction of personal faith and personal choice, even if such focus on the individual was usually accompanied by signs of the influence of background and environment. Many people in the past three centuries have genuinely believed that their religious position and affiliation were chosen freely by them, while observers might have concluded that they had been under considerable influence (including the tendency to go against parental precepts, as well as the tendency to follow parental practice). The established church, or state church, remained in England and Scotland, Scandinavia and the different parts of Germany, Switzerland and the Netherlands (where more than one 'state church' existed together), and in each case, to varying extents, alternative churches were permitted, usually with a price to pay, such as exclusion from universities or from parliament. Such penalties were common through Europe until the end of the eighteenth century when the parish clergy exercised great power, involved themselves in scholarly and scientific research, and lived as gentlemen – or, those with good livings and bountiful inheritances did so. There have always been poor clergy. The parish ministry at its best, however, has represented available religious resources which turned nobody away, and regarded the entire population as its constituency. To some extent it remains, though the process of regarding the church as a community of individually chosen belief has continued.

The rise and spread of Methodism after the preaching of John Wesley may be said to exemplify, or participate in, three important elements in the changing world of Christianity in the eighteenth century. The first is the growing appeal of a 'religion of the heart'; the second the growth of alternatives to the established Church; and the third the religious fervour accompanying the opening up of the vast territory which became the USA. Wesley was born in 1703, became a priest of the Church of England, and carried out a preaching ministry of great vigour and much travel, including a brief sojourn in the American colonies. His brother Charles, who shared the work, is known best for the hymns which he wrote, some of them among the best known and loved wherever worship is held in English: 'Jesus, Lover of my soul'; 'Hark! The herald angels sing'; 'Christ the Lord is risen today'; 'Rejoice, the Lord is King'; 'Lo he comes with clouds descending'; 'O for a thousand tongues'; 'Ye servants of God, your Master proclaim'; 'Love divine, all loves excelling'. In 1795, four years after John Wesley's death, those who had been drawn together by the movement became formally a separate church, which grew in numbers rapidly, both in England, where many people involved in nineteenth-century industry were enthusiastic members, and in the developing United States, where the style and flexibility of the Methodist Church proved well suited to the westward settlement of the country and the creation of new towns.

Despite the religious intensity of some early settlers in New England, the attitude to religion of those who led the separation of the US from Britain at the end of the eighteenth century was one of broad toleration with little time for creeds, theological disputes, or dogmatic enthusiasm. The nineteenth century, however, saw the rise of churches of diverse nature – denominations – which flourished without state support and in more or less friendly competition with one another. Methodists and Baptists became more numerous than the Congregationalists (largely of New England), the Episcopalians (who retained a position as the church of the elite) and the Presbyterians (hailing from Scotland and Ulster, prizing scholarship and a learned ministry). Later, in the middle of the century, the Roman Catholic Church grew rapidly, largely the result of Irish immigration, and, with Catholics from other European countries following, the Catholic Church became the majority church in the northern states, the Baptists being the largest in the south. It took a long time, however, for Catholics to be accepted as equals in the United States. Communities of Irish, Poles, Italians and others provided shelter and encouragement to these groups, with the church offering religion and social service – and, not least, making marriage outwith the Catholic fold exceptional. There was a suspicion among other church people that the Catholics were not fully American, taking their orders from Rome, while the Protestants practised a Christianity which kept alive the old sense of

America as a place and people uniquely called by God to be in special relationship to him. It was well into the second half of the twentieth century before such anti-Catholic bias could be said to be largely, if not wholly, overcome.

American Christianity (and the term has often been used without irony) has contained both dogmatic, strict phases, and periods of a more liberal, relaxed, looser approach to the faith. As nineteenth-century industry brought success and wealth to many, preachers proclaimed divine support for the American enterprise; but after some time a note of criticism appeared, in which progress was no longer welcomed without qualification, and successful citizens were urged to promote good developments and show care for people. This Social Gospel approach flourished as the nineteenth century moved into the twentieth. It taught a liberal Christianity, sympathetic to scientific and cultural development, disinclined to fight over doctrines, keen on good works – but far removed from revolutionary fervour, and with little or nothing to say about the division between whites and blacks in a country supposedly devoted to equality. Partly in reaction to the Social Gospel came Fundamentalism, with belief in the Bible as literally accurate in all details, and especially with opposition to Charles Darwin's discovery and/or theory of evolution. After the Second World War a liberal period of active church life enthused about ecumenism, but by the end of the century the limelight moved from the mainstream liberal churches to the Christian Right, with television evangelists proclaiming hostility to many aspects of modern life and promoting a strong defence of American power in the world. The United States remains a country where church attachment is considerably greater than that in Europe, including Britain, and the number of denominations can be assessed in hundreds or, if all the small independent congregations were counted, in thousands. It has produced religious groups which have augmented Christian doctrine through the contributions of their founders. Of these, the largest and best known are the Mormons, the Jehovah's Witnesses and the Christian Scientists.

In the countries of Europe, the historic home of the Christian religion from the days of Constantine, the fortunes of the Church vacillated over the past two centuries, though the general trend has been one of declining church attachment, diminishing influence of the clergy, and huge reduction in the number of people professing belief in the central doctrines of the faith. We may ask why the situation in Europe is so different from that in America, and there is no one simple answer. Churches in Europe were, by and large, provided by 'the authorities', while in the US the people freely chose to support the churches they wished to build and promote. Major intellectual scepticism about God, Christ and the Bible was widespread, but that was true of North America also. The French Revolution led to and expressed widespread hostility to the clergy, the church and Christian doctrine. When socialism enthused people with a vision of a more equal society, and one where the workers on the factory floor shared more of the profits of their labour, the churches in some places took positions of frightened hostility, while in others the movement was more sympathetically received. Where churches were established or state churches, support for the church often included an element of support for the political order, and for the monarchy; but, on the same grounds, people who resented the status quo and had little love for 'top' people might decline to support the religious arm of the establishment whose social and political arms they also opposed. The Communist Revolution in Russia and the subsequent Soviet domination of Eastern Europe, brought spasmodic, brutal suppression of the church and periods of toleration. Not surprisingly, persecution produced fervour, if not among all. In Britain, church attachment, moving up and down, has undergone a major decline in the last thirty or forty years of the twentieth century. Yet Christian worship continues to be offered throughout Europe at the beginning of the third Christian millennium, though the European churches, like Europe itself, may often give the impression of being old and tired. Moreover, the birth rate here is falling, which is not the case in Africa.

A Southern Church

At the start of the twenty-first century the Christian cause is strongest in Latin America and Africa, if strength is measured in numbers of people. There are more Roman Catholics in Brazil than in any other country in the world. The story of the Catholic Church in the former Spanish and Portuguese Empires of the west since the coming of independence in the first quarter of the nineteenth century reveals a clergy sometimes at odds with governments, sometimes supporting them, and equally in fluctuating relationship with Rome and the pope. In the two centuries of Spanish and Portuguese rule, the appointment of bishops and general supervision of the church had come from Madrid and Lisbon and their respective kings, rather than from papal Rome. (Until recently, versions of that situation were fairly common in European Catholic countries. Centralisation of such matters in Rome alone is relatively new.) Through the varied allegiances of clerics across the centuries, however, two connected elements have characterised much of the religious life of Latin America, from Mexico southward: the continuing presence of imagery, myth and ritual from the pre-Christian period, and the powerful significance of the Virgin Mary. Some people held that the period before the conquests following Columbus' voyage in 1492 was not 'pre-Christian', since according to some sixteenth-century missionaries the Apostle Thomas had established a Christian presence there shortly after the crucifixion of Christ; and, although there may be no grounds for treating the claim as history, the story may have assisted a much-needed sympathetic attitude to those customs greatly cherished by the indigenous peoples. The assumption of European and Christian superiority is no less insulting to the people who are its victims because it is unthought and taken for granted.

The enormously exalted position occupied by Mary in Latin American Christianity is fairly matched by the place she has occupied in the piety of Catholic people from early times. The Council of Ephesus in 431 declared that Mary was to be called *Theotokos* (usually translated into English as Mother of God), and the great Church of Santa Maria Maggiore in Rome was built soon after in celebration of her status – that church, incidentally, having a ceiling said to be of the first shipment of gold from the New World, presented by Ferdinand and Isabella of Spain to Pope Alexander VI. The devotional practice of the rosary, a string of beads, each reminding the user of a prayer, is said to have come from a vision in which Mary spoke to the founder of the Dominican Order in the thirteenth century and left him with a string of beads to be used when reciting the Ave Maria – the prayer based on the salutation of Mary in St Luke's Gospel by the angel Gabriel and Elisabeth, Mary's sister: 'Hail, Mary, full of grace, the Lord is with you. Blessed are you among women, and blessed is the fruit of your womb, Jesus' (Luke 1: 28, 42). The 'rosary' comes from the association with a garland of roses, Mary being regarded as 'the rose without thorns', the 'rose of Sharon', and the blood-red rose of suffering and sorrow. It is difficult, perhaps impossible, for anyone who has grown up in a culture that does not share this deep devotion to Mary to understand the intensity with which that devotion is given. It is so wide that suggestions have been made from time to time that instead of a Holy Trinity there is a Quaternity, including Mary, but these ideas tend to come from bemused outsiders. Thousands of people make pilgrimage journeys where people have reported visions of Mary. Among the most famous of these visions were those at Guadalupe in Mexico in 1531, Lourdes, France, in 1858, and Fatima, Portugal, in 1917. In May 1946, 700,000 pilgrims, almost a tenth of the population of Portugal, gathered at Fatima to give thanks to Mary for the ending of the Second World War. Pope John Paul II had great devotion to Mary from his boyhood in Poland, hailing her as Queen of Poland and testifying to her with a capital 'M' beside a cross on his heraldic shield. Hymns are regularly sung to her. If, therefore, there is added devotion in Latin America because of mother-god figures in the ancient lore of those people, that devotion is mixed with a vast widespread love of Mary stretching far beyond the shores of the Spanish and Portuguese New World.

Two ingredients in the devotion to Mary may be mentioned, as much for what they suggest of the wide scope of Christian practice as for their immediate significance. The first is that several of the testimonies to visions of Mary include her giving milk from her breast to them. That picture may offend more refined Christian people, though there may be more than one way of defining refinement; but religious people have so often been seen by others as prim and prissy, easily shocked, that it is good to be challenged by signs of basic bodily activity. The other ingredient is that, though little is known about Mary from the Bible, it would be wrong to claim that there are no biblical associations in the devotion that is paid to her. One of the themes of the rosary is that of the fifteen mysteries of Mary, each of which the person saying the rosary was expected to visualise. List them, and you will see that they are almost all taken from the Bible. Mary's Joyful Mysteries are the Annunciation, the Visitation, the Nativity, the Presentation, and the Finding of Jesus in the Temple. Her Sorrowful Mysteries are Jesus' Agony in the Garden, his

Scourging at the Pillar, his Crowning with Thorns, his Carrying of the Cross, and his Crucifixion and Death. Her Glorious Mysteries are his Resurrection, his Ascension, the Descent of the Holy Spirit at Pentecost, the Assumption of Mary into heaven, and her Coronation as Queen of Heaven. You cannot say the first thirteen of these are not in the Bible, and the last two can probably be interpreted in ways which convey meaning of some significance to those who cannot regard them as events. Such interpretation of apparent statements of fact is surely common to religion, and is practised both when the statement is regarded as factually accurate and also when it is not. One thing not to be missed in any attempt to understand Christianity is the widespread use of the Bible as a library or armoury from which phrases and images have been taken throughout the centuries for use in dealing with subjects of a wide and general nature. 'Tell it not in Gath', I remember from childhood as a way of pleading for confidentiality. It comes from David's lament for Saul and Jonathan in the first chapter of the Second Book of Samuel. When the Pope referred to Martin Luther as a 'boar out of the wood', however, he was doing more than employing convenient imagery. He was comparing Luther's assault on the Church to the misfortune overtaking the chosen people of God, which was the point of the verse in the eightieth psalm from which it was taken – 'the boar out of the wood doth waste it, and the wild beast of the field doth devour it.'

I have been using aspects of the church's life in specific places and times as pegs on which to hang references to the more widespread significance of these aspects in Christianity. Latin America is a good place to look for the central position of Mary in Christian devotion, even if it is not so among the churches described generally as Protestant. Comfort and help are associated with her, as chief among the advocates pleading for sinners before the heavenly throne. One of her titles was 'Sinners' Lawyer'. To some, that might seem to conflict with the New Testament picture of Jesus Christ as 'our advocate with the Father'. Both, however, may lead to a separation of God the Father from Christ as from Mary and the other interceding saints, as if the believer relied on the persuasive sympathy of the kindly ones to squeeze a welcome out of the cold, remote, proper and even rather ill-tempered senior One. So many of the expressions of Christian thought require to be set beside other expressions, making rather different points, so that when they are put together we get a sort of federation of ideas, or at least a three-dimensional picture.

From the late 1950s, through the following two decades, Christianity throughout the Americas produced a mood of radical social concern which went far beyond the controlled benevolence of the Social Gospel and the Catholic hierarchy's support for poor relief, while also supporting the structures of society which kept the people poor. The Civil Rights movement in the states of the USA, led by Martin Luther King among others, pressed for an end to the racial segregation which had outlived by a century the Civil War with its promise to free slaves and treat all as equal. The movement of thought from the issue of race to the wider search for freedom from oppression led to Liberation Theology, which flourished in Latin America, and brought the corporate emphasis of the Bible to balance the individualism of the modern world. A good community is not to be defined as a community in which individuals, some or most, are personally good, irrespective of their relationship to the whole community. A good community is one with structures and safeguards devised to promote a healthy sharing of gifts and needs, with particular attention to vulnerable and needy people. More than ambulances and bandages are needed for health. Good food, clean water and exercise make the need for medicine less likely. A society which is geared to the increase of wealth among the owners of commerce and trade, with little benefit to those at the bottom of the heap, apart from occasional doles of emergency relief, is not a good society, from the perspective of the Liberation Theologians – nor, they would say, from the perspective of the Gospel of Christ. Helder Câmara, Archbishop of Olinda and Recife in Brazil, famously said 'When I feed the poor, they call me a saint. When I ask why they are poor, they call me a Communist.' Marxist terms and concepts were indeed used in the analysis and programmes of Liberation Theology, and it met with considerable opposition from conservative elements both at home and in Rome. The theologian Gustavo Guttiérrez wrote, 'Sin occurs in the negation of man as brother, in the oppressive structures created for the benefit of the few and for the exploitation of peoples, races, and social classes.' [*Theology of Liberation*, translation (Maryknoll, NY 1973), pp. 175-6.] Church people around the world have been learning, though it should not have been forgotten, that forgiveness of sin involves more than private release from individual guilt. It also means new beginnings in communal responsibility, and the restructuring of frameworks to make freedom and equality more likely, locally and globally. The flame of these ideas has been suppressed, though not extinguished, in the closing years of the twentieth century, not least by the policies of Pope John Paul II and the bishops he appointed in Latin America. Yet such insights will not go away. It is, after all, fully three centuries since John Donne wrote:

No man is an island, entire of itself; every man is a piece of the continent, a part of the main. If a clod be washed away by the sea, Europe is the less, as well as if a promontory were...: any

man's death diminishes me, because I am involved in man-
kind, and therefore never send to know for whom the bell tolls,
it tolls for thee. (*Devotions upon Emergent Occasions*, No. 17.)

Liberation Theology may be seen in part as a reaction to the
evangelical form of Christianity which flourished in revivals and
missionary endeavour towards the end of the eighteenth century and
the beginning of the nineteenth, and gave fuel to the missionary
movement throughout that century and well into the twentieth. It
emphasised the universal nature of sin, the need for personal
repentance, the acceptance of Jesus as Lord and Saviour, and the
living of a pure and holy life. Structures and the reshaping of the
community were not significant, except to the extent to which changes
were thought to encourage personal piety and morality.

Africa was the great field where souls were to be won for Christ, and
missionaries lived and died to spread the Gospel on the huge continent.
North Africa had, of course, been significantly Christian before the rise
of Islam. The Coptic Church in Egypt remains in continuity from the
days of the Apostles. A successful mission operated in the Kingdom of
Kongo from the late fifteenth century for at least two centuries. Nubia
had a strong Christian community in the Middle Ages, and Ethiopia has
a Christian tradition dating back 1,700 years. The rest of Africa, south of
the Sahara, was evangelised in the nineteenth and early twentieth
centuries, and soon showed signs of developing a distinctly African form
of the religion which both held to the historic faith and expressed itself in
African ways. Prophets and seers, healers and liturgists, took from the
indigenous tradition and re-expressed it in Christian terms. The Old
Testament featured strongly, and the ethos of Sabbath-keeping Jews
became commoner in Christian Africa than in Christian Europe or in
America, north or south. It took a long time before a positive gratitude
for pre-Christian African religion could be expressed, but in the late
twentieth century Archbishop Desmond Tutu of Cape Town was able
to say that 'It is reassuring to know that we have had a genuine
knowledge of God and that we have had our own ways of
communicating with deity, ways which meant that we were able to speak
authentically as ourselves and not as pale imitators of others. It means
that we have a great store from which we can fashion new ways of
speaking to and about God, and new styles of worship consistent with
our new faith.' The number of Christians in Africa grew from 10 million
in 1900 to 360 million in 2000. Africa and Latin America can be
described as the new heartland of the Christian faith.

A Family of Customs and Opinions

It has been estimated that the proportion of the world's population which can be regarded as Christian will be roughly the same in 2050 as it was in 1900, namely just over a third (34%). The majority will not be European or white. Nineteenth- and twentieth-century missions have spread church membership through Africa, the Far East (notably South Korea), the Pacific Islands, and elsewhere. The church in India is large by European standards, though small in proportion to the nation's total population. In the past century Pentecostal churches, with their emphasis on the direct influence of the Holy Spirit, have grown rapidly, and it is reckoned that there will be one billion members in 2050, equal to the number of Hindus, and twice the number of Buddhists. The number of Christians in the world in 2000 has been given as 1,900 million, and the number of Muslims 1,150 million. While it may not seem so from the perspective of a Briton, or any European, it is clear that the majority of the world's people have a religious connection, and that the cause of Christianity is by no means finished.

How can we tell what they believe? Or, more significantly, how far is it possible to know the extent to which the central claims and imagery of their religion serve the practical purpose of giving a focus to their lives – their personal wellbeing and their practical priorities and conduct? Two people may be said to be praying, side by side; what is going on inside their minds and spirits? What do they think is happening? Their subsequent demeanour and the way they treat their fellows may be observed, but who can estimate the part their praying has played in making them what they are? The moral standards of Christian people – the standards they profess, that is – have been, on the whole, much like the minimal accepted standards of any society that holds together well: keeping one's word, not harming others or stealing their goods. Of course, some societies have held such to be compatible with, say, having more than one wife; but keeping such codes would matter there, and stealing others' wives would be forbidden. Claiming that Christians are loving and forgiving needs to be set beside their record, and beside the way in which people who profess other religions or none can be loving and forgiving. Christians, like others, can also disagree about when forgiveness is appropriate, and when judgement and punishment have prior claim. Christians may be described as people who worship together, with Jesus Christ as their focus, but some will go to services every day, and others every two years, and both groups regard themselves as Christian. Can we say more than that Christianity is a family of customs and opinions relating to Christian faith and worship?

As the numerical significance of Africa increases, as well as the enthusiasm gauge of the African Church, one element that becomes apparent is the greater dependence on the Hebrew Scriptures (the Old Testament) of the church in Africa. The keeping of the Sabbath, on Sunday or on Saturday, following the fourth of the Ten Commandments, as set down in the Book of Exodus, and the emphasis on prophets and inspired, ecstatic, visionary leaders, testify to that Hebrew devotion. Such attachment may also serve as a challenge to the European and Europe-influenced parts of the church to learn again some ingredients of the faith to which the Hebrew Scriptures bear powerful witness. One is the emphasis on corporate responsibility as well as individual duty. Christian people have been urged to follow certain codes of conduct and avoid other acts (not steal, not commit adultery); but there has sometimes been a large imbalance between the care taken with personal conduct and the lack of care about the life of the community. Even when interest has been shown in public matters, it can seem lopsided, as when bad language on television provokes fury among people who seem not to spare a thought for slum housing or homelessness. The Hebrew prophets reminded people forcefully of their vocation to care for the needy, the stranger, people in distress. It is true that the Ecumenical Movement of the twentieth century – the search for greater unity among churches – has brought an increased emphasis on the corporate nature of the church, which is not to be regarded as clergy-run, but instead 'the body of Christ'. One wonders, however, if the stress ought to be less on the social coherence of the church and more on the part the church can play in the social coherence and fairness of the community. At least historic Christendom and its national and parish churches made less of the distinction between church people and the whole population. Perhaps they were right. A moral perspective which does not regard personal breaking of rules, including sexual rules, as the only serious sins, but also regards financial stewardship and the quality of the whole community as equally important, and which emphasises positive duties rather than prohibitions, is something the 'old' churches need to learn.

Modern people in the developed world might also learn from the Old Testament its reluctance to restrict reference to the divine to any one word, or name. Basic belief seems, at times, to be so strongly tied to the word 'God' that generations of men and women may have been left with the idea that if they could not imagine someone who resembled a big human (usually male), but was also different from humans, they were obliged to conclude that they did not have Christian faith. Imagining God, however, has never been part of Christianity, and certainly was not part of the faith of Israel. Equally, no one name was tied to the Holy One, the creating source of life. The most sacred name was never spoken. It was written with four consonants, YHWH, and nobody knows with certainty what the vowels might have been. It was traditionally expressed in English as Jehovah, more recently as Yahweh. But when they came to it in the Bible, Jewish people spoke another word, usually 'Lord' (as they still do now). Faith is never a matter of getting the words right. White Christianity may have shackled the spiritual searching of millions by allowing them to think that 'God' was a proper name, like Churchill or Shakespeare, and that to be a believer you had to be able to imagine the one whose name it was.

Not only is the Christianity of millions of southern believers one which honours the larger part of the Christian Bible. It is also said to be nearer the religion of the first Christian centuries than Europe or most of North America has seen for many a year. While that is a difficult judgement to verify, it raises the question of modern scholarship in relation to the Bible and the faith, and its bearing on the contemporary church, in all parts of the world. The period of the Enlightenment and the Age of Reason led to critical examination of the text of the Bible, as well as attempts to express the 'true' meaning of the Christian faith through the cultural lenses of the time. Much of the most influential teaching and writing was done in the German universities in the nineteenth century. Manuscripts of the Hebrew (Old Testament) and Greek (New Testament) Bible were found and compared, so that a variety of readings was sometimes available for one phrase or verse. Most significantly, analysis of the first five books of the Bible showed them to be an amalgamation of four distinct sources, and it became generally believed that they could not have been written by Moses. That led to a new appreciation of the Hebrew Bible as a work reflecting centuries of change, and not a work dictated, as some held, by divine communication as a coherent unitary volume. Something similar happened in the study of the Gospels, when scholars formed the conclusion, now widely accepted, that the first three Gospels are closely connected, Mark being the first written, and Matthew and Luke being put together from three sources, namely Mark, another unknown source, and material peculiar to Matthew and Luke respectively. The fourth Gospel, by St John, was held to be later, and less likely to contain historically accurate material, though that view has been modified by some more recently. The Bible was opened to people in a new way, and the result was helpful to the faith of some, less helpful to others. In particular, some people felt, and some still feel, that if they could not believe that the words attributed to Jesus were definitely spoken by him, their Christian faith suffered a severe knock. For others, the more tentative witness through the mists of memory and the local environments of the early church fitted well with Jesus' own method of teaching by stories and pithy epigrams – namely, that this faith was not a matter of following details slavishly, but invited interpretation and re-expression in succeeding times and places. That is what has happened, though in recent years there have been signs of a return to the older way of reading the Bible, with specific confidence that the Gospels, in particular, are historically accurate.

One of the ways in which the culture of the time affected religious understanding was the tendency, in the nineteenth and early twentieth century, to play down miraculous elements, such as the Virgin Birth and the Resurrection, as well as Jesus' miracles of healing, and to set to one side the credal claims, such as 'being of one substance with the Father', and to present Jesus as a good man with humane ideas and a vision of a better, even perfect, world. The picture fitted the optimism of Europe before the First World War, and probably appeals to many even now, who might say that they have little time for creeds and miracles, but admire Jesus as a good man. Even before the War, the picture of Jesus offering a vision of a good life and making a good world was qualified by scholars, including Albert Schweitzer, who argued that the Jesus presented in the Gospels was not envisaging a gradual process of improvement but the early conclusion of human history. With that thinking, and the dream-shattering carnage of 1914 – 18, 'Liberal Protestantism' took a severe knock. The new mood was best represented and led by Karl Barth who emphasised the initiative of God in Christ, through the Bible, against any stress on human progress. Barth's strong position did not, however, prevent other scholars from sharing this perspective while not denying the advances of biblical scholarship. Later in the century, Roman Catholic scholars, who had been prohibited by their church from sharing the new analysis of the Bible, were allowed to do so, and many have been at the forefront of the continued study and interpretation of the Scriptures in the second half of the twentieth century. How far such scholarship reaches the person going occasionally to Sunday morning service is difficult to guess.

It is now widely predicted that the Christian majority of the twenty-first century will be conservative in doctrine and moral matters, insisting on a 'literal' understanding of the Virgin Birth and the Resurrection, even if others continue to claim that neither can be described 'literally' but were mysteries from the start. How can such different positions be reconciled? One way is separation or tolerant distance with occasional polite mutual recognition, which is no new thing. Possibly more valuable would be an increased awareness of the 'mysterious' elements of the faith as ingredients of worship more than subjects for debate or for reaching personal conclusions. The distinguished theologian saying 'I can no longer say the Creed, but I can sing it' was making my point. Religions, however, seem to have provoked many squabbles, apparently with little justification, and Christianity is no exception.

Some Questions – Some Replies

I have tried to tell the story of Christianity as it has been known throughout its long history. This is not a 'scholarly' book, with detailed footnotes and reactions by the present writer to discoveries and claims made by theologians and historians modifying or questioning widely held assumptions about what happened and why it happened. I think I have given a general survey of Christian history which is widely accepted, and the discerning reader will recognise where my own preferences have added a gloss to the story, without, I hope, distorting the facts under consideration. I have allowed humour to appear here and there – or what seemed to me to be humour, both to lighten the task of reading what I have written, and, most importantly, because humour is one of the best ways of admitting that people being deeply serious can often also be putting ideas before people and risking the destruction of good things by elevating them into something like gods.

Now, in conclusion, I would like to consider some questions which I think an inquisitive, intelligent reader may fairly be asking about this whole 'Christianity' thing. In giving some responses to these questions, I hope I may be less guarded than I have been, because I think my imagined reader deserves that I try to express more of the struggle which a professional Christian minister has with his religion, not because I think that my slant on the faith is the only right one, but, on the contrary, I believe that when many people throw their own tuppence-worth into the common pool that pool is most likely to express some balance of interpretation which no individual can possess alone. Indeed, the nearer a person comes to representing a faith of perfect balance, the more likely that person is to be less of a thinking individual, more a boring computerised entry in a religious textbook.

What is a Christian?

Almost thirty years ago I went for a walk in the hills of North Carolina with Carlyle Marney, a Baptist Minister who had been described as the most acceptable preacher on American university campuses in the heady 1960s, when students were cheerfully and passionately questioning everything. I found that he often said things which I felt, on hearing them, were things I might be about to think, but his expressing of them led me to think them and believe them to be right. One of the things he said, which he often said and had written, was 'Christian is adjective, never noun'. Since hearing that, I have felt strongly inclined to practise it in my speaking about the faith. Clearly you could dismiss the statement as rubbish. Look up a dictionary, and you will see that 'Christian' has been both noun and adjective for long centuries. Marney, however, was not trying to change the language. He was putting in shorthand form a conviction that Christian believers are never fully Christian, and none of us has reached the stage of holding all the desired Christian qualities in one life. 'Christian is adjective, never noun' is for me a helpful reminder that aspects of us from time to time may be true to our faith, but other aspects at other times will certainly be less true, or quite untrue, to it. We are like pieces in a jigsaw, in that we see the whole picture only when the pieces fit well together. That is not a reason for regret, but a ground for hope, and it may be said to be true of humanity in general. Some might even say that religion will serve the human race best when the different religions fit well together, though decent mutual respect would do quite well for a start, and that decent mutual respect among the religions of the world is practised quite a lot in today's mobile multicultural world, despite the intolerance and aggression which are so much more likely to get prominence in the media.

Much the same point was, I think, being made in a radio interview by Joseph Needham, the eminent historian of Chinese science, probably also about thirty years ago. In the last of three interviews, most of which had been taken up with questions about his life's work, the interviewer asked 'Dr Needham, are you a Christian?' His reply, as I remember it, was, 'I deplore the growing custom of singling out individuals and referring to them as "Christians". I am much more at home with the old way of calling a man a "churchman". If you ask me if I am a churchman, my answer is that I am.' Now I am not pleading for a recovery of lost usage in the English language. Customs of speech change. What has remained with me over the years is the distinction between being identified by one's individual beliefs and commitments, and being identified by one's sharing in something much larger and greater than private judgement or personal position. Even if it brings ridicule to say so, I set much store by the claim that the basic definition of 'Christian' is 'a member of the Christian church'.

It will certainly be protested by some that authentic Christian faith involves a personal commitment by an individual to Jesus Christ – and, further, that such a commitment comes out of an experience of conversion, a deep awareness of the grace of God befriending a person through Christ. I cannot disagree that that is one way of speaking about Christian faith. It seems to me, however, that a person with such a momentous experience can be expected to grow in his or her awareness of being a piece in a large jigsaw. The Apostle Paul made the point (surely with a humorous chuckle) in his First Epistle to the Corinthians (1 Corinthians 12: 14-27):

> A body is not a single organ, but many. Suppose the foot were to say, 'Because I am not a hand, I do not belong to the body', it belongs to the body none the less. Suppose the ear were to say, 'Because I am not an eye, I do not belong to the body', it still belongs to the body. If the body were all eye, how could it hear? If the body were all ear, how could it smell? ... The eye cannot say to the hand, 'I do not need you.' ... But God has combined the various parts of the body, giving special honour to the humbler parts, so that there might be no division in the body, but that all its parts might feel the same concern for one another. If one part suffers, all suffer together; if one flourishes, all rejoice together.' Now you are Christ's body, and each of you a limb or organ of it.

Therefore it seems there need be no conflict between personal faith and common, shared faith, when the former leads on to the latter.

Those who say that members of the church have done terrible things have a strong case for what they say. Through the centuries people have treated their fellows with cruelty and insult and remained leaders of the church. From the perspective of today, the past can be declared to be flawed and in part disastrous. Who knows what our successors in future centuries will say about us? It is all too easy to take the prevailing perspective of one place and one time and judge all others against it; but that does not excuse past inhumanity, or remove the evidence for some very bad things being done in the name of Christian evangelism and Christian authority.

Awareness of past failure does not of itself equip us to define what good and true Christianity is in practice. If it is not enough to say that a Christian is a member of the church, what are the qualities we expect of a Christian, a member of the church? Too often in practice the behaviour expected of Christian people has seemed to be defined negatively, tested against a list of prohibitions ('thou shalt not ...') and not enough by the call to positive qualities, which can simply be summarised by the word 'love'. To do your neighbour no harm is itself a recipe for ignoring your neighbour. What is called for is not indifference or neglect, but generosity and respect. Goodness can be made to sound more like inoffensiveness than strong generosity, and Christ may often have been presented in such a way as to justify such thoughts as the poet Swinburne's 'Thou hast conquered, O pale Galilean: the world has grown grey from thy breath' (from *Poems and Ballads*, 1866).

Christian history is full of giants whom nobody would call meek or inoffensive: Paul, Augustine, Francis, Luther, and Wesley come to mind. However, qualities of greatness – imagination, courage, determination, strength of personality – can often carry with them qualities we might not find so attractive: obstinacy, zeal reaching to ruthlessness, leadership becoming dictatorial. You do not send a mouse to lead an army. Yet without the flashing brilliance of greatness, where would any great cause have gone? It will not do to say that a true Christian has only admirable qualities. The second half of the Ten Commandments may provide a good checklist of things rightly to be opposed in a humane civilised society; but they require also the positive qualities of generosity, creative imagination, art and vision.

The historian Thomas Carlyle took the need for such an acceptance of the risks of greatness when he assessed the poet Robert Burns, with his sexual indulgence and infidelities, in these words: 'Granted, the ship comes into harbour with shrouds and tackle damaged; the pilot is blameworthy; he has not been all-wise and all-powerful: but to know how blameworthy, tell us first whether his voyage has been round the Globe, or only to Ramsgate and the Isle of Dogs' (*Essay on Burns*, 1828).

Clearly it is difficult to define a Christian by behaviour or to insist that the good qualities of Christian people are quite different from the good qualities of people who follow other religions or none. Also, while Christian people find inspiration and guidance from Jesus Christ, that does not conflict with other people finding inspiration and guidance from other sources to do things similar to the good deeds which the Christian people may do. For me, the Holy Communion, Eucharist, Mass, Lord's Supper, is both deeply practical and deeply mystical. In it, we identify in practice with the life of Christ, in breaking bread and pouring wine and sharing them with one another. We not only express in ritual form the value of giving and giving up for the good of the whole, the significance of losing to find, expending to bring new life; we also deliberately look to the life of Jesus as our inspiration and guidance. Thus we learn in depth about generous self-giving as the key to fulfilled humanity, and recognise that self-giving as the central element of life. That is what worship is, for Christian people.

I accept that it is probably inevitable that Christian people will tend to have in mind, more or less clearly, some picture of the sort of person whom they would regard as a good or true Christian, whose convictions and behaviour ideally express what the majority feel they should be, even if they have little intention of being like that completely. The picture will change from time to time and from place to place; but it will always include the observance of regular worship, the avoidance of 'bad' deeds, and an attitude of generosity and forgiveness to others. Yet the varied nature of personal qualities and the risks of expecting all the virtues to coincide in one person, especially oneself, lead me to the conclusion that it is better to look for, and work towards, a good mixture of qualities in a group, or indeed in the whole Christian community of the world, with plenty of opportunity for the strengths and weaknesses of individuals and traditions to balance, complement, and compensate for one another.

Is there such a thing as a Christian lifestyle?

For centuries, in Europe and the Americas, sexual behaviour was probably the principal area of activity by which people were judged to be living well or living badly. Premarital and extramarital sex were certainly not unknown, and in some places it was common for a man and a woman to marry only after the woman was pregnant with the man's child. In mediaeval and early modern times the concern within royal and aristocratic circles for legitimate heirs and ordered inheritance of titles and property was not replicated among the bulk of the population, among whom the social disgrace of a discovered breach of sexual 'rules' only became significant, varying from place to place, in the last centuries or so. In the nineteenth and twentieth centuries people actively involved in churches were expected to be chaste before marriage and faithful within marriage; but with the contraceptive pill becoming available in the 1960s, and the unprecedented access of women to higher education and the professions, sexual relations before marriage have become the practice of the overwhelming majority, including those who are active church members and are married in a service of Christian worship. Surveys have shown that so great is the change that couples not only no longer regard sex outside marriage as sinful: they also regard it as irresponsible to marry without first assuring each other of their sexual 'compatibility'. At the same time divorce, while not welcomed as openly as premarital sex, has become widely acceptable, and many ordained ministers, certainly in the United States, have remarried after divorce, without scandal or impairment to their acceptance in their profession. These developments do not represent an unqualified loosening of self-discipline, but in many cases a deep commitment to fidelity with one's current partner, married or unmarried, in a culture of serial fidelity combined with varying attitudes to marriage, ranging from favour, when it is good and while it lasts, through acceptance for social reasons to down-right opposition to marriage as an arrangement which carries too much baggage of male domination and the weakening of genuine affection and romance.

It appears that the wider Christian community reflects the prevailing culture of its time and place, in sexual as well as other areas of behaviour. There is usually a minority who follow a stricter code, though some would say that even among them there is considerable departure from the expected standards, if with greater secrecy and concealment. The Christian religion has been so integrally bound up with society as a whole in many countries that one is driven to suppose that either authentic Christian behaviour is the choice of a small minority or that the minority ethos is an unattained ideal or an inevitable exception.

There has also, I believe, been a judgement by many that thinking about morality was in the past focused too much, and too exclusively, on matters of personal behaviour, and sexual behaviour in particular. The health of the community, the quality of housing, the provision of educational opportunities, and the proportion of national income spent on armaments have come to be seen as moral matters as much as personal behaviour is; and the responsibility of the whole world for the whole world has been asserted as a deep matter of right and wrong. It is a topsy-turvy moral sense that condemns me for taking apples from a neighbour's tree while having no interest in what my country does about the accumulating debt of Third World countries or whether I derive regular income from shares in the tobacco industry. It is a cock-eyed morality which gets worked up about profane language on television while taking no interest in people sleeping rough in shop doorways. If our Christianity moves us to think about right conduct, our thinking needs to cover more than a few items of behaviour, and corporate and communal decisions need to be included, at least as high on our list of duties as not stealing from shops or orchards, and avoiding fights on the street.

Do you have to believe in God to be Christian?

That will strike some people as a silly question. They will say that the answer is obvious, that without belief in God Christian commitment is totally impossible. Much, however, depends on what is meant by 'believe in God', and many people may possibly be put off committing themselves to church membership because they cannot bring themselves to go along with what they think belief in God involves. I would like to make four points, in an attempt to offer a helpful response to the question.

It appears to me to be likely that there are many people who assume that the clergy, or most of us, and the people who are thought to be the most convinced and committed, have some clear notion of God which is somehow denied to the less committed, the searchers on the fringe. They may think that we can close our eyes tight shut and have in our minds a picture, either like that of a friend living far away whom we have not seen for years, or like an imaginary creature, such as a unicorn, which nobody has seen, but which it is possible to imagine. I even suspect that children have been encouraged to include God in a world of fantasy, make-believe, or science fiction; and some people are better than others at letting their imagination run wild and cook up some improbable contraption, which then becomes part of their fantasy life and which they would regard it as disloyal to ditch. If so, these leaps of the imagination, clever as they may be, have nothing whatsoever to do with Christian or Jewish belief in God. It is true that writers, in the Bible especially, have written of God doing such things as seeing and speaking, which make him sound like a human person; but they have also written of him as being like a bird ('under his feathers shalt thou trust'), which has not led believers to pronounce that God is, in fact, a bird. To take elements from events and behaviour which we know and use them to sketch out something of the mystery to which the word God points is one thing. To say that God *is* one or other of such images is quite another. It is true that the writers of Genesis spoke of God creating man in his own image and likeness, and it is possible that other biblical writers thought of the human physical form as having something in common with a divine physical form; but alongside these writings there is a huge reticence about describing God, and it is fair to say that while humans may have something which resembles some aspects of God, it is quite another thing to take aspects of humans and try to paint a picture of God, or define God. We may be content with noting that the alternative to saying nothing at all about God may be the use, tentatively and with reverence, of aspects of things seen on earth, including people, in order to say something, at the risk of letting poetic suggestiveness be taken as factual description. For me, and, I think, for many, the use of 'like' in the phrase 'humans are like God' is quite different from its use in 'donkeys are like horses'. Our inability to describe God, and therefore imagine him, is my first point.

The second point is that ideas and images which are used to talk about God may be closely bound up with aspects of human behaviour which are dated and even offensive from the perspective of many people today: words such as king, reign, lord, majesty, footstool, and even servant, with its association with a class system of a past age. People may get over their difficulty with imagining a superhuman and accept that that is not what they are being asked to do. They may then face the next hurdle of being invited to use words and images which suggest a mediaeval king's court or a desert chief's camp fire. Even if they can bear the thought of using these terms without being committed to their 'normal' use in human society, the question remains: are they being asked to adopt towards the Divine One the attitude of palace flunkeys to an absolute king, or of camel drivers to a desert sheik? Is prayer a cringing activity? I know that for some I may appear to be inventing a problem where none exists. I reply that I have overheard people on a rare visit to church for a funeral grumble over all the references to 'the Lord', and from my knowledge of them I am sure the objection came from their socialist politics. It matters to me that Christian faith should not be presented in a way that seems biased against such a standpoint. I suspect we are lazy about revising our imagery, though some hymn-writers have been creative in that direction.

Thirdly, as I have tried to say earlier, belief in God is not so much an opinion that there is somebody called God as the exercise of a certain sort, or quality, of trust. I might even make the suggestion, dangerously as it may be, that in the words 'worship God' the word God may be regarded as acting as an adverb, indicating that the worship is fundamental, referring to everything and to a oneness giving unity to all the bits and pieces of reality. Such worship or trust is better described as a relationship with a person than as a focus on wholeness or some such; but this is not meant in the ordinary sense of relationship, like a person's friendship with another person. In practice, that is what seems to happen in worship or prayer. The language of talking to a Father is better than any other way of doing it; but it remains a huge mystery, and is not the same as talking to one's father or mother. I know that what I am saying may be puzzling or offensive, or both. I am, however, trying to be helpful, and I am also sure that though wise people who live with the imagery of a heavenly Father can use it with assurance, there are others who are prevented from a spiritual activity in which they would like to engage because they cannot get round what they see as factual claims, instead of treating them as fragile frameworks in a mist of metaphor.

The fourth point, so important for Christian believing, is that Jesus Christ is the 'image of the invisible God' (Colossians 1: 15). To believe in God in a Christian way is to focus your attitude of worship on Christ, and that is much more what Christian worship means than trying to imagine a Superior One somewhere or nowhere. To worship via Jesus Christ is to identify the wholeness or oneness of all life with him, to identify the fundamental standards for human living with him; and to identify him with the mystery of grace, liberating help coming from outside ourselves, calming and restoring us, befriending us towards freedom, celebration, and service.

The essence of a Christian belief in God is not the imagining of a superfigure in the sky or anywhere. To regard Jesus Christ as fundamentally and universally significant is to have what matters about belief in God, whether or not you use the word. Words are important, but they are at best aids to believing, not substitutes for it. (I say that as one who is happy to use the word God, and happy to say I believe in God, but unhappy when a word on its own becomes an insurmountable obstacle to worship and Christian allegiance.)

How can going to church mean more to me?

I can readily think of people who are drawn to the Christian religion but find church services distinctly unappealing. They would probably agree that you cannot expect to find in every church a space sensitively arranged, with order and beauty, or first-rate musicians, or clergy who positively exude holiness and humanity, with poetic use of language and sermons that stimulate mind and inform helpfully and provocatively. Some people might say it is surprising that the quality is as high as it is. Others might echo an English bishop who remarked some years ago that he found the services in the churches of his diocese so boring that he was surprised, not by how few people went to church, but that anybody at all went. Also, people's culture has changed. Television alone represents a massive change in how people are entertained, informed, drawn into political and other controversies. People attend meetings less frequently than when nineteenth-century politicians addressed tens of thousands. The singing of hymns may be the only group singing to which people are invited or exposed, when not so long ago singing round fires and in halls was common. Even when the circumstances seem propitious you may just not feel like entering into the atmosphere as you think you are expected to do, and all sorts of issues in a busy life may be rushing around your mind, utterly inhibiting calm and contemplation. For all such, and others, here are some considerations put forward in good faith.

Never despise the value of a good habit, carried out with unexamined regularity, and not requiring a specific decision to adhere to it on any particular day. People at the present time may place overmuch confidence in sincerity, a quality which can at times be in itself neutral, in that it is fine when we are sincerely wise or right, less fine when we are sincerely foolish or wrong. To decide to go to church when you feel like it, and not go 'merely out of habit', may leave your participation in worship at the mercy of the weather or of what you had to eat and drink the night before. A child may regard an occasional visit to a favourite aunt as a great treat, relishing the food which the aunt has prepared, while simply accepting mother's cooking every day as just what happens, but the latter is much more significant for the child's nourishment than the former. There is much to be said for churchgoing as a staple diet, rather than a great treat on special occasions.

Don't go to church for your own benefit only. Even when the benefit you seek is noble and spiritually faultless, consider the possibility that your presence may add to the encouragement of others present, who may receive comfort and strength in difficult times partly because of the presence of others, including you.

Some people need time to prepare for an important event. To rush at the last minute, or even after the service has begun, possibly using your mobile phone between the car and the door, could scarcely be further removed from an earlier era, when Saturday evening was different because the next day was Sunday, and a slow walk to the church was followed by quiet sitting in one's pew in good time before the service. These days may never return. Some may switch from bustle to meditation in the twinkling of an eye. Others may need several twinkles.

Remember how frail the exercise is, the one in which you are sharing. The words are not definitive, the judgements are provisional, the truth is glimpsed, not seen head on. The Welsh poet and priest, R. S. Thomas, wrote this poem, which says something deeply important about the fragile nature of worship:

> Prayers like gravel
>   Flung at the sky's
> window, hoping to attract
>   the loved one's
> attention. But without
>   visible plaits to let
> down for the believer
>   to climb up,
> to what purpose open
>   that far casement?
>   I would
> have refrained long since
>   but that peering once
> through my locked fingers
> I thought that I detected
>   the movement of a curtain.

R. S. Thomas, Folk Tale, *Experimenting with an Amen*
(London, Macmillan Ltd., 1986, p.53) © Kunjana Thomas 2001

By chance I once heard R S Thomas give a radio talk, only part of which I heard. I remember him saying something like this: 'Often on my walks I come across a hare. The hare is a nimble fellow, and usually hides himself before I reach his place. But I feel the nest he has made, and I can tell by how warm it is how recently he has been there. Perhaps that is as near as we get to the knowledge of the presence of God.' People who would like clear statements about religious themes, and irrefutable experiences of spiritual reality, might usefully learn from such a remark, and muse on the tentative nature of our hold on such areas of life. It seems to me that clear strong statements of belief and clear strong statements of disbelief tend to have in common the lack of that recognition that our statements about the divine are more like stabs in the dark than like measurements of an object you are getting ready to ship across the world. There is a verse in a hymn which I enjoy singing:

> I grasp thy strength, make it mine own,
>   My heart with peace is blest;
> I lose my hold, and then comes down
>   Darkness, and cold unrest.
> Let me no more my comfort draw
>   From my frail hold of thee,
> In this alone rejoice with awe –
>   Thy mighty grasp of me.

> John Campbell Shairp (1819 – 85),
> ''Twixt gleams of joy and clouds of doubt'.

A church service – and doubtless other events and activities – can have the great effect, and probably the great purpose, of assisting the restoration of balance, in several ways. Some aspects of our lives can be emphasised in daily work, and others allowed to take a back seat. Worship can help restore the balance. We can also be reminded of our membership of the whole human family, and that can be particularly important when daily work and natural selfishness can make us think of our group as the only important one, and put competitiveness above co-operation and the sharing of earth's joys and burdens. We can also be strengthened in our sense of the continuity of life through the generations, and see things less in the perspective of one lifetime, more from the sense of life as a river, from which one generation or one lifetime cannot be extracted or seen as separate.

The value and benefit of going to church are not to be estimated or measured, and certainly not immediately. I remember a minister proposing that people gather after service to discuss his sermon. One man, an accountant by profession, responded by saying that if he were to have anything worth saying about what he heard on Sunday, it would be Thursday at least before he would be able to say it. I do not conclude that discussions after church services are wrong, or that ready responses are invariably facile and unreliable. I simply repeat that the impact of worship may be deep and lengthy, and even the wisdom of an early appreciation may be less significant than the unspoken blessing of a lifetime's habit of devotion. You cannot say to everyone who lights a candle at a shrine, 'Now what did you get out of that?'

How can I learn more about Christianity?

Books and books continue to pour out, encyclopaedias and commentaries, studies on specific doctrines and periods, biographies and poetry, and books of meditation. Three works of comprehensive reference are:

> Raymond E. Brown, Joseph A. Fitzmyer and Roland E.
> Murphy (eds.), *The New Jerome Biblical Commentary,* London,
> Geoffrey Chapman, 1989.

> F. L. Cross and E. A. Livingstone (eds.), *The Oxford Dictionary
> of the Christian Church,* 3rd edn, Oxford University Press,
> 1997.

> Adrian Hastings (ed.), *The Oxford Companion to Christian
> Thought,* Oxford University Press, 2000.

For thoughtful studies on aspects of history and belief by contemporary scholars, the Cambridge Companions to Religion are valuable. Two I have found helpful are:

> Colin E Gunton (ed.), *The Cambridge Companion to
> Christian Doctrine,* Cambridge University Press, 1997.

> Markus Bockmuehl (ed.), *The Cambridge Companion to
> Jesus,* Cambridge University Press, 2001.

Styles of church worship and life vary enormously. It might be good to attend a variety of churches, including Orthodox and Pentecostalist, and to share something of the life of a monastery. Practice and being undogmatic are important.

Other helpful books are:

> Keith Ward, *Christianity: A Short Introduction,* Oxford: One
> World, 2000.

Alister McGrath, *An Introduction to Christianity*, Oxford: Blackwell, 1997.

N. T. Wright, *Who Was Jesus?*, London: SCM, 1992.

J. R. Porter, *The Illustrated Guide to the Bible*, Oxford: Oxford University Press, 1995.

R. Connors and T. T. McCormick, *Character, Choices and Community: The Three Faces of Christian Ethics*, New York: Paulist, 1998.

Paul Bradshaw (Ed), *The New SCM Dictionary Of Liturgy And Worship*, London: SCM, 2002.

David Self, *High Days and Holidays: Celebrating the Christian Year*, Oxford: Lion, 1993.

Alister McGrath, *Christian Theology: An Introduction*, Oxford: Blackwell, 2001.

Paul F Knitter, *Jesus and the Other Names*, Oxford: One World, 1996.

Karen Armstrong, *The Battle For God*, New York; Alfred Knopf, 2000.

Frederick W. Norris, *Christianity: A Short Global History*, Oxford: New World, 2002.

W. H. C. Frend, *The Rise of Christianity*, London: Darton, Longman and Todd, 1984.

Alister McGrath, *The Future of Christianity*, Oxford: Blackwell, 2002.

Index